AF719835

The Men's **Adult ADHD** and Anxiety Workbook

Cognitive Behavioral Therapy Skills to Manage Stress, Find Focus, and **Reclaim Your Life**

N O A H J . N O L A N

© Copyright 2025 - All rights reserved.

All rights reserved. Total or partial reproduction of this work by any means or process, including reprography and digital processing, and the distribution of copies by rental or public lending, is strictly prohibited without the written authorization of the copyright holders, under the penalties established by law.

ISBN 978-9916-781-94-4

Note: This book was created with the intention of providing information, suggestions, and guidance on various areas of life, including emotional well-being, mental health, personal growth, and the development of healthy relationships. However, it is in no way a substitute for professional medical care or the advice of a qualified psychologist or therapist. If you are facing serious mental or emotional health issues, we recommend that you seek professional help immediately.

Contents

I HAVE SOMETHING SPECIAL FOR YOU!

Do you want to be among the first to read my next book... completely FREE?

Just scan the code below and join my readers' club.

Inside, amazing surprises await you: early access to my latest releases, free audiobooks, signed copies, and many more gifts!

1

INTRODUCTION

The story repeats itself. You've been here before, and once again that same feeling runs through you from top to bottom. You're sitting at your desk at work, staring at the screen with a mind full of noise but no direction, perhaps overwhelmed by the weight of responsibility. Or maybe you're at home, surrounded by your loved ones, who sense an undercurrent of frustration in you—who realize that something isn't quite right, even if they can't pinpoint exactly what's wrong. You try with all your strength to shake off the feeling, to dismiss it by convincing yourself it's just another bad day, just one more. But deep down, you know these moments aren't mere passing discomforts; they reflect an ongoing, daily struggle with ADHD and anxiety.

Let's look at Mark's story. A software engineer and father in his forties, Mark often finds himself caught in a whirlwind of thoughts and emotions. At work, he battles a flood of distractions that rob him of focus and productivity, leaving him frustrated and drained by the end of the day. At home, Mark struggles to disconnect, to truly be present while trying to spend quality time with his family, all the while chased by a constant hum of worry—about unfinished tasks or those still to come, threatening to trip him up. Over time, he's learned to hide his struggle behind jokes and small talk, but inside, he wrestles with a persistent fear of not measuring up.

If any of this feels familiar—if you see yourself in Mark's story—welcome. You're in the right place, and most importantly, this will help you find a way forward. This workbook was created with you in mind, designed to offer a way to understand and regain control over your life.

We will get started with grasping a clear understanding of what ADHD and anxiety mean, particularly how they uniquely impact you. The societal pressure to constantly perform can exacerbate these conditions, creating a cycle of stress and perceived inadequacy. You are not inadequate.

Many myths have surrounded ADHD and anxiety, and it's crucial to dispel them. Perhaps you've heard that ADHD is merely a lack of willpower, or that anxiety is just excessive stress. These misunderstandings do little to help your struggles. Instead, it builds on your shame and avoidance instead of understanding and healing.

This workbook aims to cut through the noise, inviting you to explore the root of these challenges rather than avoiding them. Instead of seeing them as insurmountable obstacles, we'll explore how to manage them realistically. You'll learn to recognize patterns that contribute to your anxiety and scattered focus, and you'll develop strategies that actually work, allowing you to create new, healthier ways of thinking and responding to what life puts in your path on a daily basis.

We're diving into cognitive behavioral therapy (CBT) because it offers practical tools to confront negative thought patterns head-on. Because when you actively challenge these thoughts, you can begin to reshape behaviors in a way that instills confidence and peace. And who doesn't want that, right?

I want to equip you with a toolkit designed specifically for the challenges you face, tools you'll tailor to fit your life, not the other way around.

Within these pages, you'll find real-life stories from men who've faced similar trials, who've managed to channel their inner chaos into strengths. We'll look at their successes, not as blueprints to mimic exactly, but as inspiration. Their stories are proof that growth and stability are indeed possible, and that every step forward brings you closer to a calmer mind and a more fulfilled life.

As you move into this workbook, each chapter will guide you through exercises designed not only to inform but to engage you directly. These are more than checklists; they are opportunities to practice self-discipline, to cultivate emotional regulation, and to strengthen your capacity for coping with stress. As you complete them, envision building a personalized strategy that grows alongside your needs.

The goal here isn't perfection, nor is it a promise that anxiety and ADHD will vanish overnight. It's about providing a framework within you, allowing you to manage life's demands more effectively. It's about reclaiming parts of yourself that may have felt lost to the disarray of distraction or the fog of anxiety. With patience and persistence, you'll find yourself reconnecting with core aspects of who you are, allowing you to approach relationships and goals with renewed clarity. Within these pages, you can expect to:

- Understand how ADHD and anxiety uniquely impact men, including how these conditions often overlap and influence behavior, emotions, and relationships.

- Learn how to use CBT to break negative thought patterns and build healthier habits for managing ADHD and anxiety.

- Discover real techniques to reduce daily stress, replace shame with self-compassion, boost focus, and increase productivity, even when your brain feels scattered.

- Build emotional awareness and confidence, with step-by-step guidance to manage emotions and tackle fears head-on.

- Create lasting self-acceptance and resilience while growing personally and strengthening your relationships along the way.

Remember, this life and this path you are on is yours. While the outlines of each strategy and exercise are universal, how you apply them rests in your hands. Take them and the insights offered and mold them into a lifestyle that complements your unique rhythm. Celebrate all of your wins, embrace setbacks as learning experiences, and above all, grant yourself grace throughout the process.

It's time to actively shape your life story while managing your symptoms. Welcome to the beginning of reclaiming your life, one focused, mindful step at a time.

Let's get started.

2

Understanding ADHD and Anxiety in Men

Let's get one thing straight right from the start: you are not lazy, weak, or broken. You're not a screw-up or a lost cause. What you're dealing with—ADHD and anxiety—is real, and it's affecting your life in ways that go far beyond "just being distracted" or "stressing too much. If you've ever found yourself mentally checking out mid-conversation or treated procrastination like it's your full-time job with benefits, or lied awake at night overthinking everything from last Tuesday's awkward text to the meaning of life—yeah, you're in the right place.

This chapter is about peeling back the layers and making sense of what's really going on inside your mind. ADHD and anxiety often show up together, especially in men, but they don't always look the way you might expect.

You're not here to stay stuck. You're here to take your power back. And that starts by seeing the full picture—your brain, your behaviors, your emotions—not as flaws, but as things you can work with. You'll learn how to name what you're feeling, notice what's fueling your stress, and most importantly, begin creating new ways to respond with intention, instead of reaction.

Let's dive in with curiosity, clarity, and a whole lot of respect for what you've already made it through. You've been surviving. Now it's time to start thriving.

Symptoms and Challenges Specific to Men

It's not just "how you are"—it's how your brain is wired. And you're allowed to talk about it.

Most guys don't grow up learning how to spot the signs of ADHD or anxiety in themselves. Instead, we're told things like "pay attention," "try harder," or "stop overreacting." So when the symptoms show up like missed deadlines, messy desks, or overthinking everything, you might just chalk it up to being a "scatterbrain," a "hothead," or "just bad at adulting." Sound familiar?

Common Symptoms of ADHD in Men

ADHD in men often flies under the radar. That's partly because it doesn't always look like bouncing off the walls. For a lot of men, ADHD shows up as:

- **Inattention:** You meant to reply to that email... three days ago. You lose your keys again, and now you're late again. You sit down to do one thing, but three hours and eight YouTube videos later, you forgot what that one thing even was.

- **Impulsivity:** You blurt things out in meetings, spend money you didn't plan to, or jump into projects without thinking them through.

- **Restlessness**: You feel like there's a motor running inside you. You're pacing, tapping your leg, or switching tasks constantly—anything to not feel still.

Many men don't recognize these as symptoms. They just think, "That's just how I am." But that's the thing, when unmanaged, these patterns can make you feel like a failure. It's not your personality, it's your brain doing what it's wired to do. And recognizing that? That's powerful.

Anxiety Manifestations in Men

Anxiety in men can be sneaky. While we tend to think of anxiety as worrying or panicking, for a lot of guys, it comes out as:

- **Irritability:** You snap at your partner over something small. Or someone cuts you off in traffic, and suddenly your heart's racing, and you're shouting at the windshield.
- **Avoidance:** You procrastinate, cancel plans, or steer clear of anything that feels overwhelming, even if it's important.
- **Over-control:** You overthink everything. You try to plan for every outcome. You feel like if you let your guard down, everything will fall apart.

But society often tells men to be "strong" or "stoic," so instead of saying, "I'm anxious," you might say, "I'm just stressed," or worse, not say anything at all. That silence can isolate you, and that isolation feeds the anxiety.

When ADHD and Anxiety Collide

ADHD and anxiety don't just coexist; they gang up on you.

Imagine for a moment that your ADHD makes it hard to focus, so you forget to do something important. Cue anxiety:

- What if they think I'm incompetent?
- What if I lose my job?
- Why can't I just get it together like everyone else?
- Am I always going to be this scattered?

Suddenly, your mind spirals. You start overthinking every little thing—replaying that email you forgot to send or the meeting you spaced on. Then comes the avoidance. You put off the next task because your brain's already sounding the failure alarm. And eventually, you land in the self-blame zone, beating yourself up like it's your side hustle.

It's a nasty cycle. ADHD makes it easy to miss things, and anxiety makes it hard to forgive yourself. Together, they create this exhausting loop: mess up, panic, freeze, shame, repeat.

And you might not even realize both are fueling the fire. You just know something feels off. You're constantly trying to catch up, constantly questioning your worth, and constantly wondering when—if ever—you'll feel like you're doing okay.

The Stigma Men Face

Let's talk about the elephant in the room: stigma. For a lot of men, opening up about mental health feels like breaking some unspoken man-code. We've been taught to "man up," "deal with it," and definitely not ask for help. But that script? It's outdated and dangerous.

Stigma keeps you quiet when you're struggling. It convinces you that therapy is weakness. It tells you that needing support is something to be ashamed of. But truthfully, the bravest thing you can do is face what's going on inside you and take steps toward change.

Recognizing the impact of ADHD and anxiety isn't a weakness—it's your first move toward strength.

The Impact on Personal and Professional Life

When ADHD and anxiety ride shotgun in your life, they don't stay politely in the passenger seat. They grab the wheel. And while you may be doing everything you can to keep it together, it can feel like you're driving all over the road, dodging one stressor and then the next, never quite feeling in control. Let's take a real look at how these conditions can impact your world, and most importantly, how awareness is the first step toward change.

Work Performance Challenges

You sit down at your desk, ready to tackle that report, and suddenly it's three hours later, you've reorganized your email inbox, watched a video about Viking architecture, and still haven't started. Can you relate?

For many men with ADHD, focus is fleeting, and deadlines feel like moving targets. Combine that with anxiety whispering, "What if you fail?" and it becomes a perfect storm of procrastination and panic. You want to perform well. You want to be reliable. But when your mind is bouncing around like a pinball, it's hard to follow through.

It's no surprise that most men don't feel safe talking about this at work. Maybe you fear being seen as incompetent, lazy, or "not leadership material." So instead, you try harder, push yourself past your limits, or silently crumble under the pressure. The result? Stress. Burnout. And sometimes, giving up on goals you're more than capable of achieving.

Impact on Relationships

ADHD and anxiety don't clock out when you leave work—they come home with you, settle in at the dinner table, and quietly wedge themselves between you and the people you love most.

Maybe your partner says, "You're not even listening to me," and you are trying, but your mind is darting in ten different directions, chasing unfinished to-do lists and mental tabs that won't close. Maybe you forget important dates like anniversaries, school events, that one thing they really asked you to remember. Not because you don't care, but because your brain got derailed again.

Sometimes, you bottle everything up. You don't have the words or the energy to explain what's going on, so it builds and builds, until it explodes. Maybe sharp words, regret, and silence follow. And then shame.

Anxiety pushes you to pull away. You cancel plans, avoid difficult conversations, shut down emotionally—not because you don't want connection, but because you feel like a burden. Like if you let them in, they'll see the chaos inside. ADHD can lead to impulsive comments or reactions that land wrong. And suddenly, your closest relationships feel more like landmines than safe spaces.

Over time, the cracks deepen. Tension grows. Misunderstandings pile up. You may start to feel like you're failing—not just at work or with time management—but at being a partner, a parent, a person someone can count on.

And here's the part no one likes to say out loud: There's a real risk that this might cost you everything that matters. Your partner grows distant. Your kids start tiptoeing around your moods. Home stops feeling like home.

That fear—that heartbreak—is a heavy burden to carry. The idea that your brain, the way it fires and misfires, could rob you of your most precious relationships? It's overwhelming. It can make you feel helpless, or worse—hopeless.

But I'm here to tell you that once you begin to understand how ADHD and anxiety show up in your life, you can take your power back. You can name what's happening. You can explain it. You can start showing up with more intention, more compassion, and more clarity.

You can rebuild trust. Reconnect. Create space for love again—not perfect, but real.

Self-Esteem Struggles

Let's talk about the voice in your head—the one that says, "Why can't you just get it together?" That's not your intuition talking. That's shame.

ADHD and anxiety can create a loop of feeling like you're always behind, never enough. You compare yourself to others, see what they accomplish, and wonder why everything feels so much harder for you. Over time, that self-doubt chips away at your confidence and your sense of worth.

Here's the truth: low self-esteem doesn't come from who you are. It comes from years of mislabeling your struggles as "laziness," "weakness," or "flaws." When you learn to name what's really going on, you can start changing the way you see yourself and finally stop being your own worst critic.

Coping Mechanism Misuse

When you don't have the tools to manage your symptoms, you reach for something. That might be alcohol, drugs, gambling, overworking, scrolling for hours, or even total emotional shutdown. You're not trying to cause harm; you're trying to find relief.

But here's the trap: those quick fixes don't solve the problem, they bury it. And over time, they make things worse. The goal isn't to shame yourself for coping. It's to replace the stuff that's keeping you stuck with strategies that actually move you forward.

There are better ways to handle stress, regulate your emotions, and quiet your mind. As you move through this workbook, you'll learn how to build them, step by step.

Breaking the Stigma: Normalizing the Experience

Talking about ADHD or anxiety as a man can feel like breaking some unspoken rule. You may have been raised to keep things to yourself, to be the rock, to "man up" and move on. So instead of talking about how overwhelmed you feel, you laugh it off. You tough it out. Or you bury it deep, hoping it goes away.

But that silence is part of the problem. And the only way we start healing—for ourselves and for each other—is by breaking it.

Understanding the Origins of Stigma

So, where does this stigma come from?

From the time we're kids, most boys are taught that emotions are a "female thing," that asking for help is weak, and that mental health struggles mean something is "wrong" with you. Crying? Too soft. Talking about your feelings? Too vulnerable. Saying you're anxious or can't focus? Not tough enough.

But these ideas? They're outdated. And they're hurting men. They keep guys suffering in silence, pushing through pain, and missing out on the chance to get real support. By understanding where these messages came from, you gain the power to challenge them.

Mental health is part of being human. ADHD and anxiety don't make you less of a man. They just mean your brain processes the world a little differently. And that's okay.

The Power of Open Dialogue

Every time one guy speaks up, it creates space for another guy to say, "Yeah, me too."

When you talk about what you're going through—whether it's in therapy, with a trusted friend, or in a support group—you're not just helping yourself.

You're helping break the cycle. You're showing other men that it's safe to talk, safe to feel, and safe to heal.

Open conversations reduce isolation, validate real emotions, and build bridges where there used to be silence. The more we speak up, the more we normalize the fact that mental health struggles are not rare—they're common. And you're not alone.

Male Role Models Breaking the Mold

Need proof that vulnerability and success can coexist? Let's look at some powerful male voices changing the game:

- **Dwayne "The Rock" Johnson:** He has openly talked about his struggles with depression and anxiety, proving that even the most physically strong men can face emotional pain and come out stronger (GMA Team, 2023).

- **Michael Phelps:** The most decorated Olympian of all time, has spoken about his ADHD diagnosis and battles with anxiety and depression, advocating for therapy and honest conversations

(Ehrich Dowd, 2017).

- **Terry Crews:** He has used his platform to talk about mental health, trauma, and the importance of emotional honesty, breaking the idea that masculinity means silence (Bryan, 2017).

These men show us that vulnerability is not weakness—it's courage. And when guys like you and me start being honest, it creates a ripple effect that helps others do the same.

The Strength of Community

You don't have to do this alone.

There are online forums, local support groups, peer-led spaces, and communities built just for men navigating ADHD and anxiety. Whether it's a Reddit thread, a men's mental health group on social media, or a community campaign in your area, connecting with others who get it can change everything.

These communities aren't about complaining; they focus on understanding, learning, growing, and supporting.

They remind you that what you're going through isn't weird or shameful—it's human.

Getting involved, even just by reading or listening, can begin to shift the way you see yourself. And when you're ready, you might even become the voice someone else needs to hear.

Wrapping It Up: You're Not Alone, and You're Not Stuck

If you've made it this far, take a breath and give yourself some credit. You've just looked directly at some of the toughest stuff men are taught to avoid: distraction, anxiety, low self-worth, and the stigma that says, "You're not supposed to talk about this."

And yet, here you are, talking about it (or at least reading about it), reflecting on it, and starting to understand how your mind works. That's strength. Quiet, steady, real strength.

You've seen how ADHD and anxiety can show up in your job, your relationships, and your self-image. You've explored how stigma keeps so many men silent and how breaking that silence can change everything. You've realized you're not broken, lazy, or crazy. You're a guy with a unique brain and real challenges... and, now, real tools within reach.

That brings us to the next chapter.

Because awareness is powerful, but it's only the beginning. The next step? Learning how to work with your brain instead of fighting it. That's where cognitive behavioral therapy (CBT) comes in as a powerful, practical way to regain control, find focus, and rewrite the mental scripts that have been holding you back.

So, if you're ready to stop spinning your wheels. If you're done letting anxiety call the shots. If you want to take back your time, your energy, and your confidence.

Then let's move forward.

3

Cognitive Behavioral Therapy—A New Perspective

You're not broken. You're not weak. You're not failing.

But if you're like many men living with ADHD and anxiety, you've probably been carrying around those beliefs for a long time. Maybe you've been told you're overreacting when your heart's racing and your mind won't stop spinning. You've tried to "just calm down" or "hold it together," only to end up frustrated, exhausted, and stuck in the same cycle.

That stops here. This chapter is about introducing a tool that doesn't tell you to be different—it helps you work differently with your mind. It's called cognitive behavioral therapy, or CBT. And no, it's not just some feel-good advice or a fancy acronym your therapist throws around. CBT is a skillset. A mental toolkit. A way to take back the steering wheel from the chaos.

If ADHD feels like your brain is jumping from one unfinished task to the next, and anxiety feels like a constant inner alarm system that won't shut off, CBT helps you step in as the calm, grounded leader your mind desperately needs. It teaches you how to interrupt unhelpful thoughts before they spiral. How to respond instead of react. How to spot the patterns that keep you stuck, and start changing them.

This chapter will give you a new perspective: that your thoughts aren't facts, your emotions aren't enemies, and your behavior can be something you choose, not something that just happens. Are you ready to find clarity and control?

CBT doesn't want to change who you are. The goal is to help you become who you've always had the potential to be—focused, confident, grounded, and in charge of your life again.

Let's get into it.

Understanding CBT: The Thought-Feeling-Behavior Connection

CBT starts with a simple but powerful idea. Your thoughts influence your feelings, which drive your behaviors. It's like a three-part domino setup. Knock one over, and the rest follow. Let's say you just walk in the door, and your wife is upset because you forgot (once again) to pick up milk on your way home. Your thought might be, I screw everything up. That triggers anxiety or shame, which then leads you to avoid conversations, forget more things, and feel even worse.

CBT helps you pause that process. It teaches you to question that first domino—Is that thought really true?—before it knocks everything down. It's like finally finding the "pause" button on a runaway train.

If you suffer from anxiety, CBT helps break the habit of assuming worst-case scenarios. If you have an ADHD diagnosis, it helps you catch the negative internal voice saying you're disorganized or incapable. And for both? It builds emotional clarity and mental resilience.

How CBT Addresses ADHD and Anxiety

Let's talk specifics.

With ADHD, your brain moves fast, and not always in the direction you want it to. You might forget things, lose focus, or feel like you're letting people down. CBT steps in by helping you recognize the stories you tell yourself when that happens. Those thoughts aren't just painful, they sabotage progress.

CBT helps you challenge those beliefs and replace them with realistic, supportive ones. Plus, it teaches you practical tools: breaking big tasks into smaller ones, using checklists, managing distractions—real strategies that work with your brain, not against it.

With anxiety, CBT shows you how to spot when your mind is running a marathon of "what ifs." It helps you ground yourself in reality, instead of spiraling into fear-based reactions. CBT teaches you how to reframe thoughts, shift your focus, and respond calmly, even when your nervous system wants to panic.

Bottom line? CBT gives you tools to slow down, think clearly, and act intentionally, no matter what your brain is throwing at you.

The CBT Cycle: Your Inner Operating System

Picture this:

- **Thought:** I'm going to fail this presentation.
- **Feeling:** Anxiety, dread, tight chest.
- **Behavior:** You procrastinate, avoid preparing, maybe even cancel.

That's the CBT cycle in action. But once you see the cycle, you can change it. You can insert a new thought—I've prepared well, and I've done harder things before—and notice how your emotions and actions shift with it.

Understanding the CBT model gives you the power to interrupt negative spirals before they take over. It helps you stop reacting out of fear or habit and start responding with intention. And the more you practice, the more natural it becomes.

This is more than theory. It's your mental blueprint. And the cool part? You get to redesign it.

Evidence Supporting CBT: It's Not Just Talk

I have no doubt that you want solutions that work. Not fluff or guesswork. CBT is one of the most researched and recommended therapies in the world for a reason.

Studies show CBT significantly reduces symptoms of both ADHD and anxiety (Knouse & Safren, 2010). It's considered a gold-standard treatment by mental health professionals. Why? Because it gives you actionable steps to deal with your brain, not just talk about it.

In fact, men who consistently use CBT techniques often report (Raypole, 2021):

- improved focus and productivity.
- fewer anxious episodes.
- more confidence in managing stress.
- better communication and relationships.

CBT makes you feel better and helps you function better.

Identifying and Challenging Negative Thoughts

If you've ever thought Everyone's going to think I'm a failure when you make a mistake—then you've already experienced the power of your thoughts. But truthfully, just because you think something doesn't make it true. And that's exactly where this next CBT skill comes in.

Your thoughts are not facts. They're habits, and like any habit, they can be changed.

Recognizing Negative Thoughts: Spotting the Saboteurs

When you live with ADHD or anxiety, your brain tends to filter everything through a lens of:

- not good enough
- not fast enough
- not in control

You might catastrophize (This will ruin everything), overgeneralize (I always mess things up), or personalize (It's all my fault). These are called cognitive distortions, and they're like funhouse mirrors, distorting reality and making everything look scarier or worse than it is.

Let's meet Jason, a 35-year-old graphic designer with ADHD. Every time he misses a deadline, his brain screams, I'll never be successful. I'm just not cut out for this. It's not just the missed deadline that causes the stress; it's the story Jason tells himself about it.

Once Jason started recognizing these thoughts as patterns—not truths—he took the first step toward change. You can't fix a leak you can't see. That narrative—the invisible leak—drains his energy, confidence, and focus. That's what this is about: awareness.

CBT gave him the tools to trace the leak back to its source. To stop patching the symptoms (panic, procrastination, shutdown) and start fixing the root cause, his unhelpful thoughts.

The Thought Log Technique: Catch It, Write It, Challenge It

Think of a thought log like a workout tracker, but for your brain. Instead of counting reps, you track recurring thoughts and how they make you feel and act.

Let's say you're feeling anxious and irritable after a team meeting. You jot down:

- **Trigger:** weekly staff meeting
- **Thought:** I sounded stupid. Everyone noticed I zoned out.
- **Emotion:** embarrassed, anxious
- **Behavior:** avoided talking for the rest of the meeting

After a few days of logging, patterns start to emerge. You might notice you're especially self-critical during group interactions, or that certain tasks trigger the same anxious thoughts. This insight is gold.

David, a 42-year-old sales manager with anxiety and ADHD, used to beat himself up for forgetting things during meetings. Once he started logging these thoughts, he realized how often they were rooted in fear of judgment and not actual criticism. That shift helped him begin reframing the entire experience.

Challenging Negative Thoughts: Playing Mental Detective

Once you've identified the thought, it's time to challenge it. Imagine you're cross-examining your own inner critic in court.

Ask yourself:

- What evidence do I have that this thought is true?
- What evidence do I have against it?
- Is there another way to look at this situation?
- Would I say this to a friend/my child/anyone I loved in the same position?

Back to Jason: When he questioned the belief: I'll never be successful, he realized he had completed dozens of projects, received great client feedback, and was actually running a profitable freelance business. That thought had no proof or validity. It was fear in disguise.

When you challenge your negative thoughts, you shrink their power. You reclaim control.

Implementing Positive Affirmations: Rewriting the Script

Now let's go one step further. Once you've challenged a negative belief, fill the space it left with something better.

That's where positive affirmations come in. I know what you're thinking, and no, these don't need to be cheesy mantras. Keep them clear, confidence-building reminders of your capability.

Try:

- I can handle discomfort without avoiding it.
- My past does not define my future.
- I have strategies that help me stay focused.

David started using affirmations every morning before work. This wasn't an easy adjustment for him, but over time, these phrases helped him rewire how he saw himself. He stopped bracing for failure and started showing up with a mindset of growth.

And that's the real win.

Remember this: Negative thoughts are loud, but they're not the boss. With awareness, strategy, and practice, you can learn to question, quiet, and replace them. This is the heart of CBT. It's not about pretending everything is perfect. It's about seeing things clearly and giving yourself the tools to respond with strength and self-respect.

Setting Realistic Goals for Mental Well-Being

When you've been battling ADHD and anxiety, it's easy to either set goals that are way too big ("I'll fix my entire life this weekend") or to give up on goals altogether because they've felt out of reach for too long. You're not lazy. You're not unmotivated. But when your brain is working overtime just to stay focused or regulate emotions, even everyday goals can feel like swimming in winter boots.

That's where goal-setting—done the right way—can change everything. This isn't about perfection or hustle culture. This is about building structure, momentum, and confidence with tools that actually work for your brain.

The SMART Goals Framework: Turning Intention Into Action

Let's talk about SMART goals. No, not just "smart" as in clever. We're talking S.M.A.R.T.—specific, measurable, achievable, relevant, and time-bound.

Here's what that looks like in action:

- **Unfocused goal:** I want to feel less anxious.
- **SMART goal:** I will practice deep breathing for five minutes every morning for the next two weeks.

The second goal is clear, doable, and trackable. You're no longer hoping to "just feel better"—you're creating a real plan that supports progress.

Why this works for ADHD and anxiety:

- It reduces overwhelm by giving your mind structure.

- It creates tangible success points to build momentum.
- It increases accountability, especially if you write it down or track it visually.

Let's talk about Marcus.

Marcus is 39. He's a smart guy—thoughtful, creative, funny when he lets his guard down. But he's also been battling a quiet storm for years: anxiety, self-doubt, and that frustrating mix of ADHD-fueled procrastination and perfectionism.

For months, Marcus had been telling himself he needed to "get back to writing." It used to help him sort through his thoughts, especially the stuff he didn't feel like saying out loud. After a tough breakup and feeling stuck at work, the idea of writing again felt important. But every time he sat down to do it, he froze.

So he didn't write, and then he beat himself up for not writing. Classic cycle. That's when his therapist stepped in and helped him reframe the goal.

Instead of "get back to writing" (aka, an emotional minefield wrapped in vagueness), they created a simple, doable plan:

"Write for 20 minutes, three times a week, using a timer."

It didn't matter what he wrote. He could journal about his day, vent about the breakup, or jot down half-finished thoughts. The goal wasn't brilliance, it was motion. Marcus didn't need a massive transformation overnight. He just needed to start. And that small shift—writing with a timer, on his terms—became the domino that tipped the rest.

Breaking Down Goals: Progress You Can Actually See

Big goals are intimidating. "Get in shape," "Fix my marriage," or "Be more productive" are so vague, your brain doesn't know where to start. ADHD minds especially need clarity and steps.

So we break goals down.

Think of it like building a Lego set. You don't dump all the pieces on the floor and hope it becomes a spaceship. You follow the steps, one block at a time.

Let's say your big goal is to build better emotional regulation.

Break it down like this:

1. Learn three grounding techniques.
2. Next, practice one technique daily for a week.
3. Then, track what works best in different situations.
4. Use your favorite strategy during moments of stress.

Each step gives you a chance to win, and every win counts.

Celebrating those small victories is essential. Whether it's checking a box, journaling progress, or telling a friend, recognition fuels motivation. And motivation keeps the wheels turning.

Monitoring Progress: Adjusting, Reflecting, Moving Forward

The best goals aren't static; they evolve as you do. That's why checking in with yourself is key.

Maybe journaling every night felt great for two weeks, but now it's feeling like a chore. That's not failure. That's feedback.

Use questions like:

- What's working?
- What feels like resistance?
- What small adjustment could make this easier?

Eli, a 45-year-old dad juggling work and ADHD, realized his goal of "meditating 15 minutes a day" was too much on busy mornings. He scaled it back to five minutes of quiet breathing before bed. That tiny tweak made it sustainable, and that's what made it stick.

Tracking doesn't have to be fancy. A calendar, habit tracker app, or even tally marks on a sticky note can keep your goals visible and your progress real.

Emphasizing Mental Health as a Priority: Because You Matter

Let's zoom out for a moment.

Setting goals for your mental well-being isn't just about checking boxes; it's a statement: I matter. My mind matters. My peace matters.

Men are often taught to power through stress, silence emotions, or equate self-worth with productivity. But real strength is building a life where your mental health isn't an afterthought—it's a foundation.

Whether you're managing ADHD, anxiety, or both, goal-setting is self-care in action. It's not about doing more, it's about doing what matters with purpose.

Try this: Set one small goal for the next seven days. Make it SMART. Break it down. Track your progress. Celebrate it. This isn't about proving anything to anyone else. It's about showing up for you—consistently, intentionally, and powerfully.

Wrapping It Up: Your Mindset Is Your Momentum

If you've made it this far, take a breath and take a bow. You've just taken a huge step in shifting how you think, feel, and respond to the world. You've learned the core of CBT: that your thoughts shape your feelings, your feelings shape your actions, and that you have the power to interrupt that cycle and create something better.

You've learned how to recognize the negative thoughts that keep you distracted, anxious, or overwhelmed. You've explored how to challenge them, how to log and reflect on them, and how to start reshaping them into beliefs that support—not sabotage—you. You've even practiced setting goals that work with your brain instead of against it.

This is transformation in motion.

But insight without action is like a gym membership you never use. That's why the next chapter is where the real-life rubber meets the road.

In the next chapter, we're going to dive into tools you can actually use in the heat of the moment. Like when your thoughts are racing, when you're feeling wired or shut down, when life hits hard and fast. These aren't abstract ideas. They're everyday practices for calming your nervous system, regaining focus, and showing up like the grounded man you're becoming.

You don't need to be perfect. You just need a plan, and that's exactly what's coming next.

4

Practical Coping Strategies for Everyday Stress

If you've been living with ADHD and anxiety, you already know that everyday stress isn't just "everyday." It piles up faster. It hits harder. And it sticks longer. What others brush off as no big deal can derail your entire day, week, or longer, draining your focus, triggering frustration, and leaving you wondering if you'll ever get ahead.

I'm here to remind you that your brain isn't your enemy. You just need the right tools for your kind of wiring.

This chapter is your hands-on toolbox. No fluff. No complicated theory. Just practical, doable strategies that help you calm the chaos, stay grounded, and get back in control, even when life gets messy. I'll break down small, powerful techniques that make a real difference—how to breathe when your mind is racing, how to interrupt spiraling thoughts before they take over, and how to reset your nervous system when you're about to snap.

You'll also learn how to build routines that support your focus, create small wins that build self-discipline, and respond to daily stress in a way that strengthens your confidence—not chips away at it.

It's time to get equipped. Whether you're handling a tense conversation, stuck in traffic, or trying to resist the urge to ghost every responsibility, this chapter will help you meet stress with clarity, not chaos.

Let's start turning stress into strength. One skill at a time.

Mindfulness Exercises Tailored for Men

When your brain runs like a browser with twenty tabs open—fifteen of them blinking with urgency—slowing down might feel impossible. But mindfulness isn't about becoming a monk or silencing your thoughts. It's about noticing what's actually happening right now instead of being hijacked by stress, intrusive thoughts, or emotional reactivity.

For men with ADHD and anxiety, mindfulness can be a game-changer. It helps you reclaim your focus, reduce internal chaos, and respond—not react—to what life throws at you. Here are three practical, no-nonsense mindfulness exercises designed to fit into your day and your lifestyle:

Walking Meditation: A Move Your Body Kind of Mindfulness

This isn't about walking in circles while chanting mantras. It's about turning something you already do—walking—into a way to anchor your mind in the present moment.

Step-by-step:

1. Start walking at a natural pace. No need to slow down unless you want to.

2. Notice your feet. Feel the pressure as they connect with the ground.

3. Bring attention to your surroundings. What do you see? Hear? Smell? Name a few things in your mind.

4. When your thoughts drift (and they will), gently bring your focus back to your steps or what's around you.

5. Breathe naturally. Sync your breath with your stride if it helps calm your pace.

Why it works:

- Gets you out of your head and into your body.
- Combines movement and mindfulness, which is ideal for restless minds.
- Easy to slip into commutes, walks around the block, or errands.

Body Scan: A Full System Check for Stress and Tension

This technique brings awareness to your physical body, helping you catch and release tension before it becomes overwhelming. You don't need to sit in silence for 30 minutes, five will do.

Step-by-step:

1. Sit or lie down somewhere comfortable. Close your eyes if you can.

2. Take a deep breath. In through the nose, out through the mouth.

3. Start at the top of your head. Notice any sensation—tightness, warmth, or nothing at all.

4. Slowly move your attention down your body—forehead, jaw, shoulders, chest, arms, belly, hips, legs, feet.

5. At each point, ask: "Is there tension here?" If so, breathe into it and let it go.

6. End with a few deep breaths. Feel the weight of your body supported by the ground.

Why it works:

- Helps you recognize where stress hides in your

body.

- Promotes physical relaxation, even in the middle of a busy day.
- Can be done in bed, at your desk, or during a short break.

Mindful Eating: Your Plate, Your Presence, Your Peace

Instead of eating like you're racing the clock, this practice slows things down so you can actually enjoy your food and your moment.

Step-by-step:

1. Pause before your first bite. Take a breath. Notice the colors, textures, and smells.
2. Take a bite slowly. Focus on the taste and how the food feels in your mouth.
3. Chew deliberately. Count a few chews if it helps keep your mind from drifting.

4. Put down your fork between bites. Check in with your hunger and fullness.

5. Avoid multitasking. No phone, no TV—just you and your meal.

Why it works:

- Builds a stronger connection to what and how you eat.
- Reduces mindless eating and supports better digestion.
- Turns everyday meals into pockets of calm and presence.

Try this: Choose one of these exercises today. Not all three. Just one. Start where it feels easy and real—not perfect. Over time, these small anchors will help you handle stress better, sharpen your focus, and feel more at home in your own body.

You're not here to escape your mind, you're here to master it.

Deep Breathing Techniques for Immediate Relief

Stress doesn't always wait for the right time to show up. It hits in meetings, on commutes, mid-conversations, or just when you're trying to fall asleep. And when your nervous system goes into overdrive, the first thing that changes is your breath.

Learning to control your breath is like having a remote for your stress response. It's one of the fastest, most powerful ways to calm your body and regain focus. You don't need equipment, there is no noise, and no one even has to know you're doing it.

Here are four deep breathing techniques that are simple, fast, and effective when you need immediate relief:

4-7-8 Breathing: The Nervous System Reset

This method uses structured timing to ease your body into a relaxed state, slowing your heart rate and easing anxiety.

Step-by-step:

1. Sit or stand with your back straight.

2. Inhale through your nose for 4 seconds.

3. Hold your breath for 7 seconds.

4. Exhale slowly through your mouth for 8 seconds.

5. Repeat the cycle 4 times (or more if needed).

Why it works:

- Calms your fight-or-flight system fast.
- Promotes a sense of balance between effort and release.
- Can be done discreetly anytime, such as before a presentation, during traffic, before a difficult conversation, or even lying in bed.

Box Breathing (Square Breathing)

Used by athletes, first responders, and even Navy SEALs, this technique is ideal when your anxiety needs a strong, grounded counterbalance.

Step-by-step:

1. Inhale through your nose for 4 seconds.
2. Hold your breath for 4 seconds.
3. Exhale through your mouth for 4 seconds.
4. Hold your breath again for 4 seconds.
5. Repeat this box shape for 4–6 rounds.

Why it works:

- Gives your mind a rhythm to focus on instead of racing thoughts.
- Ideal for moments when you feel overwhelmed or out of control.
- Creates an instant anchor in chaos.

Diaphragmatic Breathing (Belly Breathing)

When you're anxious, your breathing becomes shallow. You will notice that your chest rises, your shoulders tense, and your brain gets less oxygen. This technique brings your breath back to its natural powerhouse: the diaphragm.

Step-by-step:

1. Place one hand on your chest, the other on your belly.

2. Inhale deeply through your nose for four seconds. Focus on expanding your belly, not your chest.

3. Exhale slowly through your mouth for six seconds. Let your belly fall gently.

4. Repeat for five to ten breaths, focusing only on the rise and fall of your belly.

Why it works:

- Activates the parasympathetic nervous system (your "rest and digest" mode).

- Improves oxygen flow and reduces muscle tension.

- Helps identify areas of tightness you can release with breath.

Guided Visualization With Breathing

When your external world feels overwhelming, visualization offers a mental retreat. This technique pairs breathing with imagery to shift your focus from stress to serenity.

Step-by-step:

1. Close your eyes and take a deep breath in. Inhale for four seconds.
2. Picture a calming scene. For you, this might be a quiet beach, a forest trail, or a favorite memory.
3. Exhale for six seconds while imagining tension leaving your body.
4. With each breath, build the scene: hear the sounds, smell the air, feel the environment.
5. Stay with it for three minutes, using your breath to guide the experience.

Why it works:

- Creates a powerful mental shift away from

immediate stressors.

- Enhances creativity and self-awareness.
- Can be done during short breaks, before sleep, or while seated at work.

Pro tip: These techniques are skills, not magic tricks. The more you practice them, the more automatic your calm response becomes. Keep a note in your phone, on your desk, or by your bed to remind you which one works best in different situations.

With each breath, you're not just calming your mind. You're building discipline, self-awareness, and control over your body's stress response. That's real power.

Understanding and Overcoming Work-Related Stress

Work can be one of the biggest sources of daily stress, especially when you're managing ADHD and anxiety. Deadlines stack up, emails pile in, distractions derail progress, and expectations (both real and self-imposed) can feel like a ticking time bomb.

If you often feel like you're sprinting just to stay in place, you're not alone, and you're not weak. You're human. And there are tools that can help you regain control.

Identifying Stress Triggers

Stress at work usually doesn't come out of nowhere. It builds—quietly and predictably—often from the same sources. The more you know your stress triggers, the better you can prevent burnout before it happens.

Try this reflection exercise.

Take a few minutes to write down your answers:

- What situations at work consistently make you feel anxious, overwhelmed, or irritated?

- What time of day do you feel most stressed?

- Are there specific people, projects, or tasks that spike your tension?

- How does your body react when you're stressed (tight jaw, racing heart, headaches)?

Why it matters:

- Pinpointing stressors allows you to create better strategies, like blocking out tough tasks during your peak energy hours or setting limits on communication with toxic coworkers.
- Patterns reveal power. When you know the "when" and "what," you can reclaim the "how."

Time Management Strategies: Structure Equals Freedom

When you live with ADHD, time can feel slippery. One task turns into ten tabs. A two-hour job becomes an all-day scramble. But with a system in place, you can stop reacting to time and start using it as a tool.

Try this prioritization strategy:

- List everything you need to do today.
- Label each task with one of these:

1. **A** = Must be done today
2. **B** = Important but not urgent
3. **C** = Nice to get done, but not critical

- Start with one "A" and don't switch until it's complete.

Use these tech tools to support you:

- **Todoist:** Create categorized task lists with reminders.
- **Toggl:** Track how you're really spending time.

- **Forest:** Stay focused by growing a virtual tree (perfect for visual motivation).
- **Clockify:** Log hours and keep ADHD wandering in check.
- **Notion:** Build personalized dashboards for goals, calendars, and projects.

Why it works:

- Prioritizing gives structure to chaos.
- Realistic scheduling reduces guilt and overwhelm.
- Apps provide external accountability when internal focus slips.

Setting Professional Boundaries

Overcommitting at work often comes from a desire to prove yourself or avoid conflict. But saying "yes" to everything is a fast track to burnout. Boundaries protect your energy and reinforce your self-respect.

Try this script for setting boundaries: "Thanks for thinking of me. I'm at capacity right now and want to make sure I give my best to the tasks I've already committed to."

Other ideas:

- Block "focus time" in your calendar, even if no one asks for it.
- Avoid checking email outside of set hours.
- Say no to meetings without a clear agenda or role for you.

Why it works:

- You can't pour from an empty cup. You need to take care of you before others.
- Boundaries help others know what to expect from you.
- Protecting your bandwidth allows you to actually enjoy your work again.

Seeking Support

Stress thrives in silence. When you open up about your experience, you create space for connection, solutions, and relief.

Try this conversation starter: "Hey, I've been feeling a bit stretched lately. Could we check in on my workload and see if anything can be adjusted?"

Or, if you're comfortable: "I live with ADHD and sometimes need clarity on priorities, can we make sure I'm aligned on what's most important?"

Why it matters:

- Talking about stress reduces shame.
- You model emotional intelligence in the workplace.
- Small conversations can lead to big improvements in workload, support, and expectations.

Work doesn't have to be a battlefield. With the right tools, boundaries, and support, you can change stress into structure and performance into pride.

You don't need to be superhuman. You just need to be strategic with the energy you have.

Wrapping It Up: From Stress to Strength

You've just taken a powerful step toward mastering stress—not by avoiding it, but by learning how to face it with clarity, calm, and control.

You've explored how to ground yourself with breath, how to use mindfulness as a daily anchor, and how to spot the invisible patterns of workplace pressure before they steal your peace. You've learned that stress isn't a weakness; it's a signal. And now, you've got the tools to respond instead of react.

Every time you pause to breathe...

Every time you walk mindfully or eat with awareness...

Every time you say no to protect your energy...

You're not just coping. You're reclaiming your power.

But stress management is just the beginning. The next chapter is where we go from calm to sharp. From surviving the chaos to owning your focus. Because once you've learned to quiet the noise, you can finally hear what really matters, and give it your full attention.

Get ready to unlock strategies that help you sharpen your thinking, stay on track, and boost your productivity.

5

ENHANCING FOCUS AND PRODUCTIVITY

Noah always had ideas. Great ones. Half-finished novels, business plans scribbled on napkins, and a garage filled with half-built furniture projects. But no matter how hard he tried to get organized or stay on task, something always pulled his attention elsewhere. A text. A sudden urge to research Viking history. The smell of coffee. Anything.

By noon, he'd already fought a dozen battles with distraction. Some he won, but most, he didn't. Then the guilt would sneak in—the kind that whispers, "Why can't you just get it together?" That voice was louder than any alarm, more persistent than any to-do list.

If you've ever sat down with a clear plan, only to realize an hour later you've gone down three internet rabbit holes and somehow started reorganizing your sock drawer, this chapter is for you.

ADHD doesn't mean you lack ambition, intelligence, or drive. It means your brain processes attention and time differently. And when anxiety gets added to the mix, it's like trying to run a marathon wearing cement shoes, with fireworks going off in every direction.

The goal of this chapter is not to turn you into a productivity machine. The intention is to build habits that help you follow through, not just start strong. It's about taming the mental noise, creating systems that work with your brain (not against it), and training your focus like a muscle.

Noah didn't need to become a different man to get things done. He just needed to learn how his brain works, create rituals that supported that rhythm, and stop measuring himself by everyone else's blueprint.

By the end of this chapter, you'll be better equipped to direct your energy where it matters most and build momentum that lasts.

Let's clear the fog and get focused.

Self-Organization Techniques

Staying on top of responsibilities with ADHD and anxiety needs to center around building smart systems. Think of self-organization as your mental home gym. The equipment might feel foreign at first, but once you get the hang of it, it starts working for you, not against you.

Let's check out some techniques that make your daily chaos feel more like a controlled mission than a surprise ambush. These aren't just productivity hacks—they're sanity savers.

Task Lists: The Daily Blueprint

You don't need to write a novel; you just need a plan. Task lists help move your priorities out of your head and onto paper (or screen), where you can see them clearly.

Your Mission Brief Exercise

- **Step 1—Write it down:** Each morning (or the night before), list three tasks that are truly important. Keep it short. If everything is urgent, nothing is.

- **Step 2— Break it down:** Take one of the tasks and list the micro-steps. For example:

1. "Organize garage" becomes:

2. clear out the left shelf

3. toss broken tools

4. label bins

- **Step 3— Prioritize:** Mark what must get done today, what can wait, and what feels optional.

- **Step 4— End of day review:** Circle what you completed. If something didn't get done, don't guilt-trip yourself. Move it to tomorrow or drop it if it's no longer relevant.

Pro tip: Keep your list where you'll actually see it, like the bathroom mirror, phone lock screen, or your dashboard—whatever works for your brain.

Time Blocking: The Focus Ritual

If task lists are your blueprint, time blocking is how you build the house. Instead of just hoping you'll get to something, you give it a home on your calendar.

The Tactical Time Map Exercise

- **Step 1—Pick your core tasks:** Use your list from above and choose two things to time-block.
- **Step 2—Assign time slots:** Use a digital calendar or notebook to block off chunks like this:

1. 9:00–9:30: review emails
2. 10:00–11:00: work on project
3. 11:00–11:15: break/stretch/snack

- **Step 3—Protect that time:** It's time to turn off notifications, shut the door, or put on headphones. That hour belongs to one thing only.

- **Step 4—Build in breaks:** ADHD brains thrive in bursts, not marathons. Block breaks as seriously as meetings. You need space to recharge.

Bonus tip: Experiment. Some men focus best in 25-minute sprints (Pomodoro). Others prefer 90-minute deep dives. Track what works for you.

Decluttering Workspaces: Clear Space, Clear Mind

Clutter isn't just physical; it's also considered mental noise. Whether it's piles of paper or 47 open Chrome tabs, disorganization quietly steals your focus.

10-Minute Reset Ritual Exercise

- **Step 1—Choose one zone:** Start with your desk, toolbox, desktop folders, or even the front seat of your car.
- **Step 2—Set a timer for 10 minutes:** Toss, wipe, sort. No perfection needed, just progress.

- **Step 3—Personalize it:** Add something that energizes you—a photo, quote, funny mug, or favorite playlist.

- **Step 4—Schedule it:** Block a weekly 10-minute declutter time. Think of it as oiling the machine.

Mindset shift: A tidy workspace doesn't mean picture perfect. It means less mental drag and faster starts.

Reminders and Alerts: Your Digital Wingman

Let your phone help you manage tasks so your brain doesn't have to do it all alone. Reminders can gently nudge you back on track when life gets chaotic.

Strategic Reminder Setup Exercise

- **Step 1—Choose a reminder app:** Google Calendar, Todoist, Apple Reminders. Pick one of these and focus on what feels intuitive.

- **Step 2— Set three core alerts:** Examples:

1. "Take meds" –8:00 a.m.

2. "Start workout" –5:30 p.m.

3. "Prep for tomorrow" –9:00 p.m.

- **Step 3—Customize timing:** Do you focus better in the mornings? Midday? Set reminders when you're most likely to follow through.

- **Step 4—Keep it gentle:** Use friendly or motivating tones:

1. "Time to crush that report!"

2. "This next hour is yours!"

3. "You got this—deep breath, begin."

Final note: Don't overload your alerts. Too many, and your brain will tune them out. Keep it minimal and meaningful.

You don't need a military-level plan to stay organized. All you need is a system that respects how your mind works. When structure becomes a support instead of a stressor, you'll be amazed at what you can build.

Small wins stack up. Let these techniques anchor your day, reclaim your focus, and help you move from scattered to steady. You've got the tools. Now let's build the routine.

Prioritization Methods

When everything feels urgent, nothing gets done. ADHD can blur the lines between what truly matters and what's just loud. That's where prioritization comes in—it's the skill of separating signal from noise.

Let's focus on doing what matters most. With the right tools, you can stop spinning your wheels and start gaining traction where it actually counts.

The Eisenhower Matrix: Urgent vs. Important

If you've ever jumped into a task just because it felt pressing, only to realize it wasn't that meaningful—this tool will shift your perspective.

The Eisenhower Matrix helps you visually sort your tasks into four categories:

Eisenhower Power Grid Exercise

- **Step 1—Make a task list:** Write out everything on your mind—big or small.
- **Step 2—Sort into the matrix:** Ask yourself two

questions for each task:

1. Is this urgent?
2. Is this important to my goals, relationships, or well-being?

- **Step 3—Act accordingly**

1. Urgent and Important: Do it today
2. Not Urgent but Important: Schedule it for this week
3. Urgent but Not Important: Delegate or minimize if possible
4. Not Urgent and Not Important: Let it go

Key insight: Urgency screams. Importance whispers. Train yourself to listen for what truly moves your life forward.

The ABC Method: Rank and Respond

This simple system helps cut through overwhelm quickly. Write out your list. Assign each task a letter:

- **A = Must do** (high consequence if not done)
- **B = Should do** (helpful, but not critical)
- **C = Nice to do** (optional, feel-good tasks)

Work through your list in this order:

1. Complete A-tasks first, no exceptions.
2. Move to B-tasks only after the A-list is clear.
3. C-tasks are extra, so don't feel guilty if you don't get to them.

Reflect at the end of the day: Ask yourself, What felt urgent but turned out to be less important? What added the most value? Over time, you'll notice patterns, like what becomes urgent, usually started as important and got ignored.

Weekly Review Sessions: Your Reset and Refocus Ritual

Life changes quickly. That's why weekly reviews are essential because they give you a chance to adjust your plans without losing momentum.

Treat your review session like a check-in with your future self.

The Weekly Reset Exercise

Step 1: Review the past week

- What did you complete?
- What got missed, and why?
- What drained your energy? What gave you energy?

Step 2— Reevaluate priorities: Use either the Eisenhower Matrix or ABC Method to plan the coming week.

Step 3—Set three top priorities: Choose the key tasks that align with your personal or professional goals.

Step 4—Celebrate wins: Take a moment to acknowledge your progress, no matter how small. Consistent effort builds momentum.

Build this review into something you enjoy. It could be done during a quiet morning walk, over coffee, or as part of your Sunday evening routine.

Prioritization isn't about doing everything perfectly—it's about doing the right things consistently. These tools help you stop reacting to every fire drill and start leading with purpose.

By focusing on what truly matters, you reduce stress, sharpen your decisions, and start building a life that reflects your goals—not just your distractions.

Creating Distraction-Free Environments

You can have the best intentions and the clearest task list, but if your environment is full of noise, notifications, and constant interruptions, your focus doesn't stand a chance. When you are trying to manage your ADHD and anxiety, your workspace matters. A lot.

Distraction isn't just about chaos around you—it's often about what's pulling your attention away from the task at hand. Let's look at how you can take control of your surroundings so your mind can finally settle in and get things done.

Identifying Distractions: Know What Knocks You Off Track

Before you fix the problem, you have to see it.

Take Jay, for example. He'd sit at his desk to work on his side business, but somehow, after checking one email, he'd end up browsing tools he didn't need, reorganizing old receipts, and researching off-grid cabins. Two hours gone, and nothing done.

Jay's real distraction wasn't just his phone or clutter; it was the lack of structure. He hadn't taken the time to identify what really pulled him away. Once he started logging what broke his focus, he realized patterns: email tabs left open, random background noise, hunger pangs mid-morning.

That awareness changed everything.

Focus Audit Exercise

When you know your triggers, you can create smarter strategies. Distraction isn't a character flaw; it's a system issue you can fix. Here's how:

- For one day, keep a quick log of what pulls your focus and when.
- At the end of the day, review it and look for patterns.
- Ask: What can I remove, reduce, or prepare for tomorrow?

Digital Detox: Break Free From the Buzz

Phones, social media, and email pings are like slot machines for your attention. And your brain is wired to check them just in case something urgent pops up.

Every morning, Leo promises himself he'll only check Instagram for five minutes. Thirty minutes later, he was watching videos on mountain biking and suddenly remembered he forgot to buy coffee. Off to the store he went. Productivity: derailed.

What helped? He created no-phone zones and set check-in times. When Leo gave himself permission not to respond instantly, his focus returned.

Phone-Free Protocol Exercise

You don't need to give up your devices; you just need them to stop owning your attention. Balance is the goal. Here's how to help:

- Choose two hours a day when your phone is either off, on airplane mode, or out of reach.
- Turn off non-essential notifications entirely. Start

with email, social media, or news apps.

- Set "tech breaks" instead of "tech bans." For example, 15 minutes after lunch and 5 minutes before dinner.

Sensory Considerations: Design for Focus

Your surroundings speak to your nervous system. Lighting, noise, temperature, clutter, all these sensory details can either soothe your mind or overload it.

Think of Aaron. He worked from home at the kitchen table, surrounded by clanking dishes, flickering overhead lights, and the constant hum of the fridge. By noon, he felt drained. He hadn't realized how much sensory stress was zapping his energy.

So he made changes: a corner desk with softer lighting, a small fan for white noise, and noise-canceling headphones. The difference was immediate.

Workspace Reset Exercise

Tailor your environment to your senses. When your body feels calm, your mind can focus. Try the following:

- **Adjust lighting:** Try natural light or warm-toned lamps.
- **Test sound:** Use noise-canceling headphones, low-volume music, or nature sounds.
- **Declutter:** Keep your desk clean and visually simple.
- **Add something calming or energizing:** Consider a plant, a framed quote, calming scents, and a clean surface.

Establishing Boundaries With Others: Protect Your Focus Time

Even if your space is perfect, one knock on the door, or a casual, "Hey, got a sec?"—can send your focus spiraling. ADHD brains don't switch gears easily. Once interrupted, it can take 20 minutes or longer to get back on track.

That's what happened to Brian. As a dad who worked half days from home, he constantly felt pulled in different directions. His kids wanted attention, the grass needed cutting, and those snacks from the kitchen were calling his name. Once he started setting up a simple signal—a supply of high protein snacks on his desk, and a "heads down" sign on the door, his family knew when he was unavailable.

It wasn't about being rude. It was about being clear.

Focus Boundary Blueprint Exercise

Learning to advocate for your needs creates not just space for focus, but respect for your goals. Give the following a try:

- Choose blocks of uninterrupted time and share them with your family or team.
- Create a signal, like a closed door, a sign, headphones, or a set routine.
- Reassure others when you'll be available again. Respect goes both ways.

Your environment isn't neutral; it either supports your focus or sabotages it. And the good news is, you don't need to overhaul your life to make it work. Small, thoughtful adjustments can help your brain settle, your tasks move forward, and your stress dial down.

Distraction is normal, but with the right setup, you can create a space that keeps you in the zone and helps you stay there longer.

Wrapping It Up

By now, you've learned that productivity isn't about being perfect or doing more; it's about doing what matters with clarity and consistency. You've explored how to structure your day with task lists and time blocks, prioritize like a pro, create an environment that works with your brain (not against it), and set boundaries that protect your energy.

These are tools to reclaim control. Every checklist, every small adjustment, every focused hour is proof: you're not just coping, you're taking charge.

But focus alone isn't enough. What happens when frustration builds, anxiety creeps in, or emotions derail your day before it even begins? That's where we go next.

In the following chapter, we'll dive into the art of staying steady in the storm. You'll learn how to understand your emotional triggers, reduce impulsive reactions, and build resilience from the inside out. Because real self-discipline doesn't just start in your calendar—it starts in your nervous system.

Let's take the next step together, toward calm, clarity, and the kind of inner strength that lasts.

6

Mastering Emotional Regulation

He'd blow up over the smallest things—a sarcastic tone in his wife's voice, the way the kids left their shoes scattered at the door, or the sink, always piled high with dishes right after he cleaned it. Traffic jams? Instant rage. He'd go from fine to furious in seconds, like a switch flipped without warning. And afterward, he'd sit with the guilt, wondering why he couldn't just let things go like everyone else seemed to.

He never meant to hurt anyone. But the outbursts were real. His wife started choosing her words more carefully, measuring her tone, shrinking around him in subtle ways. He could feel the distance growing, but couldn't quite name what was happening. He just knew they weren't laughing as much. Talking less. Arguing more. The tension sat heavy between them like static air before a storm.

Inside, Eric felt out of control, like someone else had the remote control to his emotions. And worse, he didn't know how to get it back.

Then came the gym.

At first, it was just a way to get out of the house. To get space. To feel strong in a body that felt tight with stress. He didn't talk to anyone. Just showed up, hoodie up, headphones on, and started lifting.

But slowly, something shifted. He began to notice things. His breath. The rhythm of a set. The moments his brain tried to rush ahead, but his body forced him to stay here—under the bar, in the rep, with the burn.

That hour became more than exercise. It became his practice. His quiet training ground. A place where he started to spot the early signs of frustration before they exploded. Where he learned that tension builds, and if you can catch it early, you don't have to let it wreck your day or your relationship.

He began to bring that awareness home. When he felt heat rising in an argument, he learned to pause—just for a moment—and ask himself, What's really going on here? Not to dismiss his feelings, but to understand them. To name them. To respond, not react.

His wife noticed. The eggshells disappeared. They started having real conversations again —ones that didn't end in shouting or silence.

Eric didn't become emotionless. He became emotionally strong.

And that changed everything.

This chapter is about building that same kind of strength.

Not by ignoring your emotions, but by owning them.

You'll learn how to spot your patterns. How to feel the storm coming and choose a different path. How to name what's rising in you before it hijacks your reactions. And most importantly, how to turn those emotions into fuel instead of fire.

Whether it's frustration in your marriage, anxiety in your work, or fear of letting people down—emotional mastery is what turns chaos into clarity.

You're not here to become a robot. You're here to become grounded, focused, and powerful in the ways that matter most.

Let's get into it.

Tools for Emotional Stability

When life feels like a constant pressure cooker, emotional stability can seem like a far-off goal. But the truth is, stability isn't some mystical trait you're either born with or not—it's built. Slowly. Daily. Brick by brick.

Here, I want to offer you real, everyday tools to help you stay steady in the middle of chaos. Tools that work with how your brain functions instead of against it. Think of this as your emotional toolbox. These strategies aren't fluff; they're practical, fast-acting, and made for real life.

Let's break it down.

Understanding Emotions: Name It to Tame It

Men are often taught to be stoic, which usually translates to stuffing emotions down until they come out sideways. But emotions are information. When you can name what you're feeling, you gain the power to choose your response instead of being hijacked by it.

Take Arwen, for example. He used to come home from work already irritated—his jaw clenched, mind spinning. The smallest comment from his partner could launch a full-blown argument. It wasn't until a therapist asked him, "What's the actual emotion underneath your anger?" that things clicked. He realized he wasn't just angry, he was exhausted, anxious about money, and feeling like a failure at work. Anger was just the tip of the iceberg.

When Arwen started labeling emotions more accurately—overwhelmed, anxious, disappointed—he stopped reacting and started responding. That's the power of emotional clarity.

Acknowledge your emotions without judgment. You're not weak for feeling—it's a strength to notice what's really going on.

Identifying Triggers: Know What Flips Your Switch Before It Flips You

You can't regulate emotions if you're constantly blindsided by them. That's why understanding your triggers is crucial. Triggers are situations, people, or environments that light the fuse. For guys with ADHD and anxiety, these can be quick shifts like being interrupted mid-task, loud environments, or feeling misunderstood.

Let's look at Tony. Every morning, getting the kids ready for school felt like a war zone. Shoes missing, backpacks not packed, and time slipping away. He'd blow up by 7:45 a.m. daily. But when he started tracking what set him off, he realized it wasn't really the kids. It was the lack of structure, the noise, and the feeling that he was already behind for the day.

Once he identified those triggers, he started prepping the night before, built in quiet time before the chaos, and suddenly mornings became smoother. Not perfect, but manageable.

Exercise: Trigger Tracking Map

Spend three days noticing what sets you off. Use your phone notes or a scrap of paper. Every time you feel yourself getting irritated, anxious, or overwhelmed, jot down:

- What just happened?
- Who was involved?
- What were you doing?
- What did you feel (emotion)?

At the end of three days, look for patterns. That's your personal roadmap to emotional understanding.

Journaling for Clarity

You don't need a leather-bound notebook or Shakespearean writing skills to journal. And you don't have to sit for an hour either. If you've got ADHD, attention is a precious resource. So keep it simple.

The "Two-Minute Mind Dump" + "One-Minute Check-In" Exercise

- Set a timer for 2 minutes. Write whatever comes to mind—no filter. Even if it's just "I don't know what to write." Let it flow.

- Then answer this:

1. What's one thing I'm feeling right now?

2. What triggered it?

3. What can I do about it (if anything)?

That's it. Do it before bed or first thing in the morning. Over time, you'll start to see patterns, insights, and reminders that help you stay centered.

Why it works: Studies show journaling helps reduce stress and increase emotional regulation by activating the rational part of your brain (Smyth et al., 2018).

Developing Positive Habits: Create Structure and Find Peace

ADHD brains thrive in systems, especially ones that reduce decision fatigue and increase predictability. When you create solid daily habits, you reduce the number of emotional landmines in your day.

Here's what that might look like:

- **Morning grounding ritual:** 10 minutes of movement (stretch, walk, push-ups) plus 5-minute check-in. Feel free to use the journaling tool above.
- **Scheduled recharge breaks:** 15-minute walk after lunch to clear stress buildup.
- **Nighttime reset:** Prep for tomorrow (lay out clothes, write a quick plan) to reduce morning anxiety.

A study found that those who followed structured daily routines experienced lower cortisol levels (the stress hormone) and improved emotional stability (Health Benefits of Having a Routine, 2022).

Healthy habits aren't just about productivity—they're emotional armor.

You're not expected to be perfectly calm all the time. Emotional regulation doesn't mean feeling nothing—it means having the tools to handle whatever you feel. With practice, these tools become second nature. You'll start noticing your triggers faster, managing reactions smarter, and creating a life that feels more in your control.

And it all starts with one small decision: to show up, every day, for your emotional fitness.

Learning to Ride the Waves Instead of Getting Pulled Under: Navigating Mood Swings

If you've ever felt like your moods switch faster than a playlist on shuffle, you're not alone.

For when you are diagnosed with ADHD and have anxiety, mood swings can feel sudden, intense, and frustrating, like you're killing it one moment and spiraling the next. You might not even realize it until you're already deep in the dip or riding the high. The key is learning to ride the emotional waves with awareness, intention, and tools that keep you grounded.

Let's dive into some practical ways to track, manage, and stabilize your emotional landscape even when it feels unpredictable.

Recognizing Patterns: Find Your Rhythm

Moods rarely come out of nowhere. They have triggers, environments, and patterns—although they can be sneaky about it. When you start to recognize the when, where, and why behind your mood shifts, you gain the power to predict and prepare.

Take Elijah. He noticed that every Sunday evening, he got irritable and restless. He'd pick fights with his wife or zone out with hours of YouTube. Once he mapped his moods, it clicked: it was Sunday-night dread. Work stress. That pattern helped him shift his Sundays—adding something he looked forward to, like basketball, or a meal out, which softened the emotional blow.

Exercise: 5-Day Mood Map

Using the chart below, track your mood at three points during the day (morning, afternoon, evening) for five days. Use a simple scale:

- great
- okay
- blah
- anxious
- frustrated
- low

Also jot down:

- What were you doing?
- Who were you with?
- What had just happened?

At the end of the week, look for patterns: Do your moods dip around certain times? After specific events? When you're with certain people?

Awareness is your early warning system.

Coping Strategies for Fluctuations

Once you see the mood swings coming, the next step is knowing what to do with them. You don't need a 12-step plan; you need quick, repeatable strategies that meet the moment.

Here are a few to practice:

Grounding Drill – 5-4-3-2-1

Use when emotions spike and you need to stay present. Name:

- 5 things you can see
- 4 things you can feel
- 3 things you can hear
- 2 things you can smell

- 1 thing you can taste

Grounds you in your body, not your spiral.

Cool Down Circuit

- Splash cold water on your face or hold an ice cube.
- Step outside and take 10 deep breaths.
- Do 15 jumping jacks or a 30-second wall push.

Moves the energy out of your body and resets the nervous system.

Mood Shift Menu

Make a list of five mood-shifting activities you can do anytime (e.g., walk, music, call a friend, stretch, doodle). Post it on your fridge or save it in your phone. When your mood starts to crash, pick one.

These tools get more powerful the more you use them. Don't wait until you're overwhelmed—practice in calm moments too.

Seeking Support: Connection Is Not a Weakness

Mood swings can feel isolating, but they don't have to be a solo battle. Reaching out doesn't mean you've failed. It means you're doing what emotionally strong men do: connecting. Consider:

- Texting a friend: "Feeling off today—can I vent for five?"
- Letting your partner know: "I'm in a weird headspace. Just wanted you to know I'm working through it."
- Joining a support group (in person or online) where guys talk real. Hearing "same here" can make a world of difference.

And if things feel too heavy? Therapy is a strategy, not a last resort. A place to sort out the deeper layers and get tools that fit your brain.

Engaging in Healthy Activities

One of the most overlooked tools for mood stability? Doing things you enjoy. Hobbies not only pass the time, they're also mood medicine.

Building models, working on your car, fishing, playing guitar, shooting hoops, gaming with friends (in moderation)—these aren't just "for fun." They help regulate your nervous system, boost dopamine, and keep your emotional energy moving.

Research shows that people who engage in hobbies or creative activities for just 30 minutes a day report higher life satisfaction and fewer symptoms of depression and anxiety (Rubido, 2024).

Try this: Make a list of hobbies you've loved in the past, or ones you've always wanted to try. Pick one. Schedule time for it this week. Make it as non-negotiable as a meeting.

Wrapping It Up: Emotional Mastery Is Your Foundation

You've just done what many men avoid for a lifetime—faced your emotions head-on.

You've learned how to recognize what you're feeling, track the patterns, ride the waves, and communicate without shutting down or blowing up. You've explored how journaling, grounding exercises, triggers, routines, and connection all help you stay steady—even in the middle of chaos.

Nobody is expecting you to be perfectly calm all the time. This is about knowing yourself well enough to catch the storm before it hits. To regulate without repressing. To show up in your life with clarity, with strength, and with purpose.

Every rep you put in, every moment you pause, reflect, speak honestly, or reach for a coping tool is building your emotional resilience. This is what control really looks like: not locking down your emotions, but learning how to navigate them without letting them drive the bus.

Now, it's time to take this emotional strength out into the world because while managing your inner world is powerful, facing the external world can feel just as overwhelming.

And that brings us to the next challenge: overcoming social anxiety.

Whether it's small talk that makes your skin crawl, walking into a crowded room that makes your pulse race, or the fear of being judged that keeps you silent—social anxiety can shrink your world.

But just like you've learned to regulate emotions from the inside out, you'll soon discover how to move through social situations with more confidence, presence, and freedom.

You've built the inner muscle. Now let's step into the world and use it.

Let's go.

7

Overcoming Social Anxiety

Some moments hit harder than they should.

A casual "How's it going?" can feel like a pop quiz you didn't study for. A crowded room can stir a storm inside you—racing thoughts, shallow breath, that feeling like you need to escape, now. And when the pressure's on—at work, at home, in social situations—it's easy to feel like your mind is working against you.

Take Thomas. He used to dread large family dinners. Not because he didn't care, but he cared too much. The expectations. The small talk. The feeling of being on stage without a script. Having all that extended family around at once sent his heart into overdrive. But when the arrival of his new son forced him into the spotlight, he knew something had to change.

Thomas didn't fake confidence or shove his fear into a box. He got tactical. He built a fear hierarchy—a plan to face the anxiety one small, doable step at a time. A nod. A quick hello. Making conversation with those he was comfortable with. Each win rewired his nervous system and built real, earned confidence. His fear didn't disappear—but it lost its grip.

That's what this chapter is about.

Not pretending you're fearless. Not powering through panic. But understanding your mind, learning how anxiety actually works, and building a toolkit to regain control. You'll discover how to create space between what you feel and what you choose. How to regulate emotions without stuffing them down. And how to respond to fear in a way that builds trust in yourself.

It starts with one step. Not a leap. Not a crash course in courage. Just one step toward feeling steady in your own skin.

Ready? Let's walk this through together.

Gradual Exposure Practices

Social anxiety doesn't vanish because we want it to. It softens through action—small, intentional actions that train the brain to say, I've got this. If you have ADHD, this kind of progress often comes from breaking big things into doable chunks and building momentum through experience.

Let's look at how to face your fears without flooding your system, giving you structure, tools, and space to reflect, because growth shouldn't focus solely on pushing through. It's about pacing wisely.

Gradual exposure is like strength training for your nervous system. You don't bench press 200 pounds on day one—you start lighter and increase over time. Same goes for social fears.

With ADHD, you may either avoid completely or jump all in, get overwhelmed, and pull back. Gradual exposure helps you find a middle path. Practicing low-pressure interactions and slowly increasing difficulty builds real-world resilience without burning out.

Mini Exposure Tracker Exercise

For one week, in the chart provided, track three small social interactions a day. These should be low-stakes and easy to approach. Examples:

- Say "hi" to a neighbor or barista
- Ask a stranger for the time
- Comment on the weather in line at the store

Track each one:

- Did I do it?
- How anxious was I? (1-10)
- What did I learn?

At the end of the week, ask yourself:

- What patterns did you notice?

- Was your anxiety higher or lower by the end of the week?

You'll likely notice that your anxiety didn't stay as high as expected. And you'll have evidence that you can engage—and even thrive.

Creating a Fear Hierarchy

A fear hierarchy is your personal social anxiety map. You list the things that trigger your nerves, from the least intimidating to the scariest. With this in hand, you can approach fears in order, like leveling up in a game, but for real-life confidence.

Your Fear Ladder Exercise

In the space provided, draw a ladder with 5-10 rungs. On the bottom rung, write something mildly uncomfortable, like making eye contact and saying hi. On the top rung, put a fear-inducing situation like giving a presentation to a large group.

Here's an example hierarchy:

1. Smile and say "hey" to a coworker (bottom rung).
2. Ask a question during a meeting.
3. Call to make a reservation.
4. Attend a team lunch.
5. Give a two-minute introduction during a meeting.
6. Join a networking event.
7. Deliver a 10-minute presentation (top rung)

Maybe your ladder reflects your personal life and not work. If so, it may look like:

1. Smile and say "hi" to a neighbor (bottom run).
2. Make eye contact with a cashier.
3. Attend a workshop or class with a dozen people.

4. Take your spouse on a date in a crowded restaurant.
5. Go to an outdoor festival.
6. Attend a concert. (top run).

This gives you structure. The goal is to start at your bottom rung, and as you are comfortable, you work your way up. Each level builds tolerance, and with ADHD, visualizing progress helps keep you focused and motivated.

Practical Exposure Exercises

Now that you've got your hierarchy, it's time to do the reps. Focus on one rung at a time. Only move up when you've practiced it enough that the anxiety level goes down noticeably.

Here are ADHD-friendly exposure tasks you can try. They're clear, short, and designed to create micro-wins:

Practice Set: Warm-Up Social Wins

- Compliment someone's shirt at the gym.
- Ask a store clerk how their day's going.
- Order coffee and make eye contact.

Practice Set: Conversation Builders

- Ask a coworker what they're working on.
- Share a small personal story during lunch.
- Message a friend you haven't seen in a while.

Practice Set: High-Impact Challenges

- Host a casual game night or hangout.
- Attend a local meetup or hobby group.
- Speak for three minutes in a work setting.

Tip for ADHD minds: Use a phone alarm to schedule one exposure task per day. Keep it brief—5-10 minutes max. The consistency is more important than intensity.

Reflecting on Experiences

After each exposure attempt, take three minutes to reflect. ADHD brains can forget wins quickly. Writing things down helps solidify the experience, and noticing growth keeps you motivated.

Let's look at Matthew. He was terrified of team lunches. The noise, small talk, not knowing what to say—it all made him want to ghost. But after practicing brief work chats and initiating 1:1 lunches, he finally made it to the group table. He didn't say much that first time, but he showed up, and he journaled about it.

- **Journal entry:** "Wasn't as bad as I expected. I even laughed twice. Nobody judged me. I left early, and that was okay."

That reflection became his evidence the next time his anxiety said Don't go.

Post-Exposure Journal Prompt

After each social task, jot down:

- What did I do?

- How did I feel before, during, and after?

- What surprised me?

- What would I try differently next time?

You don't overcome social anxiety in one big leap. You chip away at it. One conversation, one exposure, and one rung on the ladder. Over time, you won't just survive social settings, you'll find your rhythm in them.

Let the next step be small, but take it. That's how progress begins.

Building Social Confidence

Social confidence doesn't mean becoming the life of the party. If you have ADHD and anxiety, confidence starts with trusting yourself in the moment. It's about showing up authentically, not perfectly. It's learning to tune out the noise in your head and tune in to the connection in front of you.

I'd like to offer you real tools—not just to look confident, but to feel it.

Positive Self-Talk Techniques

It's time to start talking to yourself like someone worth listening to.

Your inner voice has power. And if it's been whispering doubts like You're awkward, or You'll mess this up—it's time to upgrade the script.

For ADHD minds, this isn't just about being "positive." It's about creating repeatable language that grounds you when your thoughts go racing or your nerves flare up. The key? Repetition, simplicity, and speaking to your progress.

Exercise: Confidence Cue Cards

Write three affirmations on index cards or a notes app. Keep the language short and action-focused.

Examples:

- "I don't have to be perfect to be valuable."
- "I can take up space."
- "I'm learning how to connect, one step at a time."

Practice ritual: Read these every morning, and again before social situations. Your ADHD brain thrives on visual and tactile repetition, so keep these where you'll see them. Desk, mirror, wallet, phone screen.

Over time, they interrupt self-doubt and ground you in your new narrative.

Mastering Essential Social Skills

Confidence is about showing you're present. Two key tools? Eye contact and active listening.

But the ADHD truth: Eye contact can feel intense, and listening can be hard when your mind's bouncing between five tabs. That's okay. These are skills, and skills can be trained.

Exercise: The Eye Contact Triangle

When speaking to someone, imagine a triangle on their face:

- left eye
- right eye
- mouth

Shift your gaze gently between these three points every few seconds. It makes eye contact feel less like a staring contest and more like a rhythm. Practice during short chats or mirror conversations.

Exercise: Repeat, Reflect, Respond

When someone speaks to you:

1. **Repeat silently:** The key word or phrase they said.
2. **Reflect:** "What do they mean?" or "Why does this matter to them?"
3. **Respond:** Ask one follow-up or offer one thoughtful comment.

This keeps you grounded in the moment, reduces the urge to interrupt, and helps you build meaningful dialogue—even if attention wavers.

Role-Playing Scenarios

Rehearse real life in safe spaces. Practice doesn't make perfect. It makes things possible. Role-playing is like a social gym because it lets you build your skills without the pressure of real-world stakes.

For men with ADHD, it's also a great way to physically and mentally prepare for situations that normally cause hesitation.

Exercise: The Social Simulator

Pick one upcoming or challenging scenario. Maybe you are meeting new colleagues, joining a group at the gym, or chatting with a neighbor.

With a friend, or even in front of a mirror:

- Play out two ways the conversation might go.
- Practice greeting, asking questions, and ending the conversation.
- Switch roles and pretend to be the other person to see it from their perspective.

1. Start small: "Hi, I'm new here. Mind if I join?"
2. Add layers: Try small talk, a joke, to help navigate awkward silences.

Every time you role-play, your brain learns the cues. You're training for real-world connection like a pro athlete trains for game day.

Learning From Role Models

Sometimes, the best way to grow is to observe how others walk through the world. Not to copy them, but to learn what confidence looks like in action.

Your role models don't need to be celebrities. They can be that guy in the office who's always calm, the friend who jokes easily, or even a character from a show you like.

Exercise: Confidence in Action Log

Pick two people you admire socially. Watch them in different interactions. Ask yourself:

- How do they start conversations?
- What do they do when things get awkward?
- Do they smile, lean in, use humor?

Write down three things they do that you'd like to try. Then, put one into practice in a low-pressure setting.

1.

2.

3.

Example: "I saw James laugh at himself when he forgot a name. It made everyone relax. I'll try that next time I forget someone's name instead of freezing up."

This is not about pretending to be someone else. It's about collecting moves until you feel comfortable making your own.

To gain social confidence, you don't need to change who you are. Instead, you will be unlocking what's already in you and giving it permission to breathe. You don't have to fake it. You just have to show up—one practiced, imperfect, courageous step at a time.

Confidence isn't the absence of fear. It's the decision to keep showing up, anyway.

Handling Judgment and Rejection

Not everyone will get you, and that's okay.

Judgment and rejection sting. Whether it's a raised eyebrow during a conversation or being left on read after a group invite, these moments can spiral fast, especially if you suffer from anxiety or have ADHD.

But here's what most people never say out loud: rejection doesn't define you. It reveals what needs strengthening. It shows where your armor is too thin and where your worth is tied too tightly to someone else's opinion.

I would like to show you how to loosen that grip and give you tools to stay solid, even when someone else's reaction isn't what you hoped for.

Reframing Negative Thoughts

What if the story in your head isn't the truth?

Social anxiety often whispers lies. "They think I'm weird." "Everyone noticed I messed up." ADHD can fuel this further by replaying moments on loop, magnifying the fear.

Reframing means grabbing those thoughts, flipping them over, and asking: Is this actually true, or just a story I'm telling myself?

Exercise: Fact vs. Fear Breakdown. Next time you feel judged, pause and write:

- What happened? (Just the facts)

- What did I assume it meant?

- What are three other possible interpretations?

1.
2.
3.

- What would I tell a friend if it happened to them?

Example:

- **What happened?** "At lunch, I shared an idea, and someone looked at their phone."
- **Assumption:** "They thought I sounded stupid."
- **Other possibilities:**
- They got a work message.
- They were distracted (not about me).
- They already knew the idea and zoned out.
- **Reframe:** "Their reaction doesn't mean my idea was bad. It means they were distracted. That's on them."

Over time, this retrains your brain to challenge automatic self-criticism and regain control over your emotional state.

Developing Healthy Self-Perception

When your confidence depends on being liked, judgment cuts deep. But when you start seeing yourself through your lens, not someone else's, it changes everything.

Men with ADHD often internalize years of criticism—being "too much," "too scattered," or "too impulsive." It's time to rewrite that inner script.

Exercise: 3-2-1 Mirror Check

Look at yourself in the mirror or jot this in your notes:

- 3 things I like about who I am
- 2 things I've improved over the past year
- 1 trait I'm proud of

Example:

- **3 things:** Curious, funny, loyal
- **2 improvements:** I follow through more; I speak up more
- **1 strength:** My energy

Doing this regularly builds internal validation, and this is something no one else can take from you. The more you acknowledge your worth, the less fragile you feel when it's challenged.

Practicing Acceptance of Imperfection

Trying to be flawless in social settings is like wearing a mask you can't breathe through. One slip and panic sets in. But your imperfections make you human, not broken.

Take Andre, a guy who stutters when nervous. For years, he avoided social situations. But one day, he was asked to play golf with some fellow dads from his daughter's school. He decided to start his morning with: "I tend to trip over words when I'm nervous, but I'm really excited to be here." The guys all shook his hand, he exhaled, and the day went great.

When you own your imperfection, it loses its grip. People don't want or need perfect, they want present.

Your quirks don't disqualify you. They distinguish you. Embracing them invites others to do the same. That's where real connection starts.

Building Coping Mechanisms

The truth? You will be rejected sometimes. It's part of life. But rejection doesn't mean you're unworthy. It means the moment, the match, or the message wasn't aligned. That's not failure. That's feedback.

The goal isn't to avoid rejection. It's to learn how to bounce back stronger.

Exercise: Rejection Recovery Map

After a tough interaction or rejection, map it out:

- What happened? (again—facts only)

- How did I react emotionally?

- What can I learn from this?

- What's one thing I did well?

- What's one small action I'll take next time?

Example:

- **Event:** I wasn't invited to a coworker hangout.
- **Emotional reaction:** Hurt, left out
- **Lesson:** I haven't really put myself out there yet.
- **What I did well:** I still smiled and was kind the next day.
- **Next action:** Initiate a casual convo with someone from the group.

Small shifts like this build resilience. You don't need to numb the sting; you need tools to process it. That's real strength.

Not everyone will see your value. Not every moment will feel like a win. But none of that gets to define your worth.

You're allowed to show up, be real, mess up, and still be enough. Judgment and rejection are detours, not dead ends.

Let them guide your growth—not guard your potential.

Wrapping It Up: You're Showing Up and That's Power

Let's take a breath and look at what you've done here.

You've faced what many men spend years trying to outrun—social fear, self-doubt, the sting of rejection, and the weight of "what if I mess this up?" And instead of hiding, you leaned in. Not by pretending to be fearless, but by learning how to act in spite of fear.

You've mapped your triggers. Practiced micro-connections. Rewrote old thought patterns. You've learned to stop giving judgment the final say, and to see imperfection not as something to fix—but something to embrace.

That's real progress. And it's yours.

Social confidence isn't a finish line. It's a muscle you're training, one rep at a time. Every small win, every awkward moment, is a brick in the foundation of your growth.

But even with all this progress, there will still be hard days. Moments you fall short. People who don't get you. Times when old patterns try to sneak back in.

And that's where we go next.

In the next chapter, we'll talk about building self-compassion and resilience—not as some fluffy feel-good idea, but as your armor. The kind that lets you recover faster, forgive yourself sooner, and rise stronger.

Because growth is about how you speak to yourself when life pushes back.

You've done the work to connect with others. Now let's strengthen the relationship you have with yourself.

8

Building Self-Compassion and Resilience

Dan used to slam the bathroom door in frustration after every argument with his wife. Not because he was angry with her, but because he was ashamed of himself. Ashamed that he couldn't just "stay calm." Ashamed that his mind would race, that his tongue would get sharp, and that afterward, all he could do was sit on the edge of the tub and whisper, What the hell is wrong with me?

Dan was 42, a father of three, and newly diagnosed with ADHD. The anxiety? That had been tagging along like a shadow for years. He thought being a good dad meant holding everything together perfectly. Instead, he found himself forgetting appointments, losing his temper, zoning out during family dinners, and then punishing himself in silence later. Failure, to him, was proof he couldn't be trusted with anything important, especially his own emotions.

But something started to change when he asked himself a different question—not What's wrong with me? but What do I need right now?

That was the turning point. It wasn't some motivational speech or perfectly executed morning routine that changed his life. It was the decision to treat himself like a person worth helping, not fixing.

This chapter is about that turning point.

It's about what happens when a man stops trying to prove his worth through perfection and starts building a foundation of self-compassion and emotional resilience instead. Not because things get easier, but because he gets stronger, clearer, and calmer.

Resilience isn't just bouncing back. It's staying rooted when the storm hits—when your thoughts spiral, your patience thins, or you lose sight of the man you're trying to become. And self-compassion? That's the part of you that says, "I can mess up, learn, and still deserve to show up again tomorrow."

In this chapter, you'll learn how to:

- Stop weaponizing your past mistakes against yourself.
- Understand how ADHD and anxiety impact your self-talk, and how to rewire it.
- Use small, daily actions to grow emotional strength without needing to be perfect.
- Recognize that being kind to yourself is a strategy.

Dan's story isn't unique. Many men like him and possibly you, have spent years fighting an invisible war inside their heads. This chapter will show you how to put the sword down and start building a life where you grow and love the life you're building. One honest, compassionate step at a time.

Embracing Imperfections and Failures

There's a moment many men know all too well. You mess up—again. Maybe you forgot your kid's field trip form (for the third time) or snapped at your partner during dinner. The guilt comes fast, like a gut punch. The mind chatter? Even faster: "Get it together. You should've known better. What's wrong with you?"

But here's the truth: Most of us weren't taught growing up: failure isn't your final truth. It's valuable feedback to help you move forward.

Understanding Growth Through Failure

Failure hurts. No sugarcoating that. But it also teaches if we're willing to listen. Every misstep holds data. Missed the deadline? Forgot your wife's birthday? Maybe your system needs work, not your character. Blew up in anger? Maybe your nervous system is overloaded, not broken.

We've been trained to fear failure like it's the final chapter, but it's actually the first draft. Resilience isn't built by never falling; it's built by rising every time we do.

Darren, a 39-year-old mechanic and dad of twins, was trying to build a side business detailing cars. He launched an Instagram page and immediately worried about judgment, so he barely posted. Then, he accidentally double-booked a client and lost a five-star review. Crushed, he considered quitting. But after talking to a friend who owned a bakery, Darren realized he wasn't alone. Every business has growing pains. So, he created a checklist system, posted his first honest "lessons learned" video, and got more client inquiries than ever. Failure became fuel.

Try this: In the space provided, write down one recent failure or mistake. Now answer these:

1. What did this experience teach me?
2. What systems (not personal traits) might help prevent this next time?
3. Who else do I know who's struggled—and grown—from something similar?

Keep this somewhere visible. Make your learning louder than your shame.

Accepting Personal Flaws

Let's be real: living with ADHD and anxiety isn't exactly a walk in the park. You might forget birthdays, get lost mid-sentence, overthink texts, or freeze up in social situations. It's easy to feel like you're always falling short. But perfection? It's a trap. And worse, it's a lie.

Accepting your flaws isn't giving up. It's stepping into reality with your eyes open and your fists unclenched.

Anthony, a 45-year-old teacher, used to dread meeting new people. He'd stumble on names, freeze up when asked questions, and leave feeling like a fraud. After moving into a new neighborhood, he decided to start his introductions with: "I have ADHD, so I might need a minute to remember your name or answer a question." Most of the new people smiled and replied, "Honestly? I can relate on so many levels." That moment cracked open something deeper—flaws don't destroy connection, they invite it.

Accepting your imperfections:

- Builds a healthier self-image (you are human, not a machine).
- Reduces internal pressure, which lessens anxiety.
- Encourages honesty in your relationships, which builds trust.

You're not here to be flawless. You're here to be real, and real is strong.

Learning From Setbacks

Every setback carries seeds for growth. It's just hard to see them when you're in the middle of it. But look back—really look—and you'll see a pattern: some of your greatest progress came right after things fell apart.

Analyzing those moments is like gathering road signs for the next leg of your journey.

Try this: Choose a setback from the past year—big or small. In the space provided, write:

- What happened?
- What did I learn about myself?

- What would I do differently next time?
- What strengths did I use to get through it?

If you're comfortable, share it with someone you trust. Vulnerability is courage in motion. And your story might help someone else feel less alone.

Developing a Growth Mindset

Resilience thrives on the belief that growth is possible. When you believe your abilities can be developed—not judged—you stop fearing every mistake. You start leaning into effort instead of hiding from failure.

You stop asking, "Am I good enough?" And start asking, "How can I grow stronger from this?"

Here's the shift:

- From "I'm not good at this" to "I'm learning how to do this better."

- From "I failed again" to "This is part of the process."
- From "I don't have what it takes" to "I haven't built it—yet."

Encouraging yourself to try again, even after frustration, is an act of power. It's how confidence is born—not in the absence of failure, but in the face of it.

Celebrating Small Victories

There was a time when Adam couldn't get out the door without forgetting something—wallet, keys, lunch, his son's soccer shoes. Every morning felt like a string of little failures. He'd start the day behind and stay there, convinced he was just "bad at life."

Then one day, his 8-year-old ran back inside and shouted, "Dad, you remembered my soccer shoes!" Adam blinked. He had remembered. No panic. No last-minute drive to school. Just a small, quiet win.

That moment stuck with him—not because it was extraordinary, but because it was different. For once, he felt capable. And that one tiny win? It kickstarted a chain reaction.

It's necessary to notice the wins that usually go uncelebrated. Because when you have ADHD and anxiety, victories often don't come with fireworks. They show up in the form of routines kept, tempers held, lists completed, or simply choosing not to give up today.

And when you start recognizing those moments—really seeing them—your confidence grows. Momentum builds. You shift from feeling like you're barely hanging on to realizing you're actually moving forward.

Recognizing Achievements

One of the biggest lies anxiety whispers is that you're not doing enough. That nothing counts unless it's huge. But progress isn't made in massive gestures—it's built in moments: replying to that email you avoided for three days, saying no to something that would've overwhelmed you, showing up when your mind begged you to hide.

Kevin, a 36-year-old graphic designer with ADHD, used to think success meant landing a big project or reaching a career milestone. But those were few and far between. What finally boosted his confidence wasn't a promotion—it was when he started giving himself credit for every day he worked a full hour without distraction. He began to see those hours as bricks in the foundation of his business. They added up. And so did his belief in himself.

Recognizing your daily wins

- reinforces the behavior you want to repeat.
- builds real, lived proof that you are making progress.
- shifts focus from failure to forward motion.

Journaling Successes

Writing things down makes them real. It gives your brain a snapshot of success, and for your unique ADHD brain, this snapshot is gold.

Exercise: Victory Vault (Nightly Ritual)

Each night, take three minutes to write down:

1. One thing you did today that you're proud of (no matter how small).
2. One thing you didn't do that you could've, and you're glad you resisted.
3. One thing you want to acknowledge about yourself.

Keep these in a "Victory Vault" journal or digital note. On days when your mind says, "You've done nothing right," flip back and remind yourself—you've already come far.

Over time, this builds a tangible record of growth. Even if your day felt chaotic, your journal will reflect resilience in motion.

Creating Reward Systems

Your ADHD brain loves rewards. Dopamine's like jet fuel. So why not use it to your advantage?

Let's take a look at some smart, fun reward ideas:

- **The 3-tier win system**:

1. A tiny win equals 10 minutes of guilt-free gaming

or YouTube time.

2. A medium win equals takeout from your favorite spot.

3. A big win equals a half-day solo adventure like a bike ride, movie, hike, or tech shopping trip.

- **Challenge coin jar:** Get physical poker chips or tokens. Each time you complete a task, drop a chip in the jar. At 10 chips? Reward time. This works amazingly well if you're visually motivated.

- **Toolbox upgrade rule:** Every time you complete a full week of habit tracking or anxiety-reduction exercises, buy a new item for your workspace or hobby area. Consider a better wrench, notebook, desk light, or guitar pedal. Growth equals upgrade.

These systems help rewire your brain to look forward to progress and make the process feel like play, not punishment.

Sharing Wins With Others

Progress kept to yourself is powerful, but shared? It becomes amplified.

Tell your partner you made it to the gym three times this week. Text your brother that you finally organized the garage. Post in a private accountability group that you cooked dinner instead of stress-snacking.

Let people cheer for you. Let them see the work you're doing to grow. When someone says, "Dude, that's awesome," it's not just validation—it's fuel.

And sharing also builds emotional intimacy. It gives your people a window into your world, and gives you a moment to be seen. Really seen. Not just as the guy who's "managing," but as the man who's showing up, trying, and stacking his wins.

Establishing a Supportive Inner Voice

Imagine having a coach who followed you around all day, saying things like:

- "You're screwing this up again."
- "You'll never change."
- "Everyone else seems to handle this just fine."

Now, imagine that coach is actually living in your own mind. That's what it feels like when anxiety and ADHD hijack your inner voice, turning it into a critic, not a companion.

When you live with ADHD and anxiety, internal dialogue can get brutally loud. It criticizes the forgotten tasks, the fumbled conversations, the flare-ups, and freakouts. And after years of that kind of inner narrative, it's easy to believe it's true.

But here's the thing: your inner voice isn't set in stone. It can evolve. It can learn to be a voice that builds you up instead of breaking you down. This chapter is about teaching that voice to become a teammate—not a tormentor.

Practicing Self-Compassion

Think about how you speak to a friend who's having a rough day. You probably don't say, "Wow, you really screwed that up. What's wrong with you?" You say, "Hey, it's okay. Everyone struggles. Would you like some help figuring this out?"

That's the tone we need to cultivate inside your own head. Because the truth is: no one benefits when you beat yourself up. Especially not you.

Exercise: The Friend Filter

When you catch yourself in a harsh thought spiral, ask:

- Would I say this to a friend I love?
- If not, what would I say instead?
- How would that shift the way I feel right now?

Practicing this daily—even if it feels awkward—starts to carve new grooves in your mental wiring. You train your brain to offer support instead of shame.

Self-compassion reminds you

- struggles are normal, not proof of failure.
- your worth isn't defined by your mistakes.
- kindness to yourself isn't indulgence—it's fuel for resilience.

Mindfulness in Self-Dialogue

Most of us aren't even aware of how we talk to ourselves. It's just a background hum of criticism, sarcasm, or dread. Mindfulness helps you tune in to that hum. To listen without judgment. To pause before reacting.

When you become aware of your self-talk, you can change it. Not by pretending everything's fine, but by offering a different, more honest message.

Exercise: Thought Pause Practice

Throughout your day, especially in moments of frustration or self-doubt, take a brief pause and ask:

- What am I telling myself right now?
- Is this voice helping me, or hurting me?

- What do I need to hear instead?

Even a one-minute check-in can disrupt the autopilot of negative thinking. That pause? That's where change begins.

Being mindful doesn't mean erasing all negativity. It means noticing your mental habits and creating space between the thought and your response.

That space is where self-compassion can breathe.

Setting Intentions for Inner Dialogue

You wouldn't walk into a workout without a plan. You wouldn't start a road trip without a GPS destination. So why leave your self-talk up to chance?

Setting an intention for how you want to speak to yourself—especially during challenges—is like choosing the tone for your inner environment.

Exercise: Morning Mantra Map

Each morning, ask:

1. What do I want my inner voice to sound like

today? (Encouraging? Calm? Patient?)

2. What situation might test me today?

3. What can I say to myself when it happens?

Write this out as a short mantra or intention. Example:

"When I feel overwhelmed today, I will say, one step at a time. I've got this."

"If I mess up, I'll remind myself, learning comes with mistakes—I'm still moving forward."

Over time, these micro-intentions turn into macro shifts. They create an emotional baseline that supports, rather than sabotages, your growth.

You're going to spend the rest of your life with your own thoughts. That voice in your head? It's your constant companion. You can't always control what happens around you, but you can guide how you speak to yourself through it.

Wrapping It Up: The Voice That Builds You

Let's take a breath and look at where you've been.

You've walked through the raw terrain of self-criticism, failure, doubt, and overwhelm. You've looked your ADHD and anxiety in the face—not to fight them, but to understand them. You've learned that being tough doesn't mean being silent, and being strong doesn't mean being perfect.

That's not small work. That's foundational. And it's the kind of work that changes lives—not just yours, but the people around you too.

Because truthfully, the way you treat yourself spills into every relationship you have. Your partner, your kids, your friends—they feel the ripple of your growth. When your inner voice shifts from not enough to I'm learning, I'm growing, I'm trying, it changes how you show up in every room, every conversation, every hard moment.

You begin to lead with self-respect. You begin to connect with honesty. You begin to live with purpose, not performance.

And that's where we're headed next.

In the final chapter, we're going to talk about achieving personal growth and fulfilling relationships—not as some perfect finish line, but as a way of living. You'll learn how to take the inner work you've done and bring it into your connections with others. To build relationships rooted in trust, growth, and joy. To set goals that matter and stick to them with confidence.

Because you're not just managing symptoms anymore. You're building something real.

Let's finish strong.

9

Achieving Personal Growth and Fulfilling Relationships

In chapter four, you met Noah. If you recall, he always had ideas. Lots of ideas.

Half-finished novels. Business plans scribbled on napkins. A garage filled with half-built furniture projects and big dreams that never quite landed. His brain was a goldmine, but also a battlefield.

Noah was at a crossroads. He was smart, creative, and deeply driven, but overwhelmed. Frustrated by how often he sabotaged his own momentum. What changed for Noah wasn't some miracle hack or quick fix. It was structure. It was choosing to change his environment, define clear objectives, build an action plan, and track his progress like it mattered. Because it did.

And he did it all with one goal in mind: to show up fully—for his work, his relationships, and most importantly, for himself.

This final chapter is about that kind of turning point.

By now, you've explored how ADHD and anxiety shape your thoughts, your emotions, your habits, and your sense of self. You've practiced skills for emotional regulation, challenged intrusive thoughts, and taken steps to reclaim control of your time and attention. You've done real work.

Now comes the part where you build on that work to grow into the man you want to become—steadier, stronger, more present, and create the kinds of relationships that don't just survive your storms, but help anchor you through them.

Personal growth isn't about becoming someone new. It's about becoming more you—with clarity, confidence, and consistency.

Let's bring it all together, so you don't just manage ADHD and anxiety, but actually live in a life you're proud to call your own.

The next step is yours.

Setting and Achieving Personal Goals: Turning Intention Into Direction

Noah used to tell himself he just wasn't a "follow-through" guy.

His ideas were always bigger than his capacity to finish them, or so he thought. But when his relationships started to suffer and his self-confidence hit a low, he realized he needed more than passion. He needed purpose with a path.

Let's take a closer look at building that path—how to set goals that don't just sit in your mind like beautiful concepts, but take root in your daily life. Goals that lead to real, visible change. Goals that feel doable, even on your most distracted days.

Defining Clear Objectives

A good goal doesn't just inspire, it gives direction.

Noah's first breakthrough came when he stopped setting vague intentions like "be more productive" or "fix my life." Instead, he asked, What does success look like in a single area of my life?

He chose his garage. Not to turn it into a workshop or a man cave, but to finish one piece of furniture and clear enough space to park his bike without tripping over old projects. That goal gave him something specific, visible, and doable.

Exercise: The "Clear + Compelling" Goal Builder

In the space provided, answer these prompts:

- What do I want to accomplish? Answer with one sentence. Be clear, not clever.

- Why does this matter to me? Connect to a personal value like freedom, peace, connection, or growth.

- How will I know I've succeeded? What will it look like or feel like when done?

- What's one small first step I could take today?

- What could get in my way, and how might I prepare for that?

Big goals can be overwhelming. But when you define what success actually looks like—down to one shelf built, one email sent, one hour blocked off—you build clarity. And clarity clears anxiety.

Creating an Action Plan

When you're easily distracted, structure becomes your superpower.

Noah took his "garage goal" and broke it into tiny steps:

- Day 1: Pick one unfinished project to complete
- Day 2: Buy the missing materials
- Day 3: Set a 45-minute timer and just build
- Weekend: Donate or recycle the rest

He even wrote these steps on a sticky note stuck to the garage light switch so he'd see it every time he walked in.

The secret wasn't perfection. It was progress with a plan.

Exercise: Map It Out "The Three S's"

- **Simplify:** What is the end result you want? Keep it basic and honest.

- **Sequence:** What are the three steps that will get you there?

- **Schedule:** When will you do each step? Attach it to a day, time, or existing habit. For example, "after breakfast on Saturday."

Tip: Add a visual anchor, like a sticky note, a whiteboard checklist, or a reminder on your phone.

Tracking Progress

When you see your progress, your brain sees a win. That builds momentum.

For Noah, tracking his progress became his personal reward system. He took photos of his garage transformation. He journaled short notes about what worked and what didn't. And on days he didn't follow through, he didn't shame himself. He got curious instead.

Tracking isn't about measuring success with a ruler. Instead, notice the journey.

Exercise: Build Your Progress Log

Each evening, in your journal, write down:

- one thing you did toward your goal (even if it was

small).

- one thing that distracted or discouraged you.
- one adjustment or insight to try tomorrow.

Bonus: Create a visual tracker, like a simple box to check, a coloring page, or a habit loop. Keep it visible.

Overcoming Obstacles

It is unrealistic to believe you can avoid problems. Instead, focus on outsmarting them.

Noah didn't stop getting distracted by coffee smells or random ideas. But he started preparing for it. He created a "Mind Parking Lot" notebook for every brilliant, irrelevant idea that popped into his head during work time. He also built in breaks—on purpose. That helped reduce the guilt spiral of I should be doing more.

Most importantly, he asked for help. His friend Joe checked in on Saturdays: "Garage progress today?" That one text helped him stay on track.

Exercise: Plan for the Plot Twist

Goals aren't just about achievement. They're about alignment. Ask yourself the following:

- What usually gets in your way? Be honest—distractions, fear of failure, energy dips?

- What can you put in place to outsmart it? Timers, accountability buddy, pre-prepped workspace?

- What will you remind yourself of when things don't go as planned? Write a mantra or post a quote that reminds you progress isn't perfect—it's consistent.

When your goals match your values and your action plan respects your brain's reality, you create something better than motivation—you create momentum.

Balancing Personal and Professional Life: How to Find Harmony Without Sacrificing Yourself

For a long time, Noah thought balance was a myth.

He believed you either crushed it at work and let your personal life fall apart, or you focused on yourself and got left behind professionally. There was no middle ground. That belief drove him to burnout more than once. Until one day, he realized the problem wasn't a lack of effort, it was a lack of strategy.

Balance doesn't mean giving everything equal time. It means giving what matters most your best energy, attention, and presence—when it counts. And that starts with intention.

Let's explore how you can start living this kind of balance in real-time.

Prioritizing Time Management

A focused mind needs a structured schedule, even if it's flexible.

Noah was notoriously bad at time. Not just being late, but chronically underestimating how long things would take. So he tried something new: time blocking.

He started using Google Calendar to map out both work and personal tasks—color-coded.

- Blue = Deep work hours
- Green = Personal goals and creative time
- Red = Non-negotiable life stuff like therapy or workouts
- Yellow = Flex time or buffer zones

He set phone alarms not just for meetings, but to start and stop working. That helped him leave work on time and be more present at home.

Tips for time mastery:

- Use time-blocking with a digital calendar like

Google Calendar, Notion, or Structured.

- Prioritize the important, not just the urgent.
- Anchor your day with a morning and evening routine; even just 15 minutes can reset your nervous system.
- Try the Pomodoro technique. This involves 25-minute work sprints plus 5-minute breaks to improve focus.

Time management isn't about squeezing more in. It's about carving time out for what counts.

Setting Boundaries

For Noah, working from home blurred everything. He used to answer emails during dinner and take client calls in bed. Eventually, it cost him sleep, energy, and even connection with his partner.

So he made changes:

- A designated workspace in his guest room.
- A sticky note on his desk: "Is this urgent or just

easy?"

- A templated email that read: "I respond to non-urgent emails between 3–4 p.m. If it's time-sensitive, feel free to call."

At first, it felt uncomfortable. But over time, people respected his boundaries—because he did.

Let's check out some strategies to establish healthy boundaries:

- **Learn to say no:** "I'd love to help, but I'm currently focused on X and don't have capacity for Y."
- **Create physical space:** If you work from home, mark "on/off" zones. On zones for working and off zones where no work is allowed.
- **Set email or communication windows:** Be sure to communicate them clearly.
- **Block personal time on your calendar:** This includes time for rest, hobbies, or date nights.

Boundaries protect your energy. And when your energy is intact, everything else improves.

Practicing Self-Care

According to the American Psychological Association, men are less likely than women to seek mental health support or engage in proactive self-care, even though they experience high levels of stress and burnout (Winerman, 2005). For men with ADHD and anxiety, this can be especially true—often tied to internalized beliefs about toughness or productivity.

Noah used to avoid self-care because it felt too indulgent. But when he hit another wall—mentally fried, physically sluggish, and emotionally shut down—his therapist gave it to him straight: "If you don't schedule your own care, your brain will eventually force a breakdown."

So Noah made three changes:

1. Daily movement—even just a 20-minute walk
2. Sunday reset rituals (groceries, laundry, and time to just think)

3. A weekly "tech-free hour" where he'd do something with his hands like paint, garden, or cook

Exercise: Create Your Personal Care Plan

You can't pour from an empty tank, and you don't need to. Consider the following:

- **Body:** What keeps you feeling strong? For instance, do you like lifting, yoga, walking, or great sleep?
- **Mind:** What gives your brain a break? For example, journaling, mindfulness, art, or reading a great book?
- **Joy:** What reconnects you to fun or flow? Do you love some good hobbies, music, sports, or games?
- Schedule each of these twice each week and treat them like important meetings.

Fostering Flexibility

Noah used to be thrown off by anything unexpected—a cancelled meeting, a sick kid, a power outage. Now, he builds "buffer zones" into his schedule and practices something he calls mental reset reps. When things don't go as planned, he asks:

- What's in my control right now?
- What can I adjust or let go of?
- What does this teach me about how I want to handle the next curveball?

Over time, those mental reps built confidence. Flexibility became its own kind of strength.

Exercise: Flexibility Framework

Flexibility doesn't mean you have no structure—it means your structure can bend without breaking. Try the following:

- **Name it:** When something shifts, don't ignore it—acknowledge the change

- **Reframe it:** Ask, What's the opportunity here? instead of Why me?

- **Reset quickly:** Don't overthink the pivot, just do the next best step.

Work and life don't exist in separate boxes. They bleed into each other, especially when you're wired for fast thoughts, deep emotion, and nonlinear rhythms.

The goal isn't perfect balance. It's intentional harmony.

Fostering Meaningful Connections: Relationships That Fuel Growth

Noah didn't realize how lonely he'd become until he finally stopped numbing his stress with busyness. For years, he'd convinced himself he was too overwhelmed for game nights, check-ins, or coffee meetups. It wasn't intentional. Life just filled in the cracks, and he let it.

But the more he got honest about what mattered, the more he noticed a gap: He was working on himself, yes. But who was he sharing that growth with?

Let's look at how to fill that space—building and nurturing the kind of relationships that don't drain you, but lift you up. Whether it's reconnecting with old friends, expanding your social circle, or finally letting people see the real you, a meaningful connection is one of the most powerful forms of growth.

Nurturing Existing Relationships

Sometimes the people who matter most are already in your life. They just need more of you.

For Noah, it started with his brother.

They hadn't had a real conversation in months. So one evening, Noah texted: "Want to grab a coffee Friday? I know I've been MIA. I want to fix that."

They talked for hours. No agenda. No pressure. Just presence.

It reminded him that relationships don't require grand gestures. They require intentional time, honest words, and simple acts of showing up.

Exercise: Strengthening Your Circle

Investing in people you already love multiplies your emotional wealth. Give one or all of the following a try:

- Pick one person you've been meaning to reconnect with. Send them a message today. Keep it simple: "Hey, I've been thinking about you. Want to catch up sometime soon?"
- Schedule regular connection time, like a biweekly call, monthly lunch, or a shared hobby.
- Write down three things you're grateful for about someone close to you. Tell them. Out loud.
- Start a "Friendship Ritual." For example, Tuesday coffee texts, Sunday memes, monthly poker night.

Expanding Social Circles

Sometimes you don't need a whole new life. You just need a few new people.

Noah joined a weekend woodworking class—not because he had extra time, but because he wanted to meet people who shared his curiosity and creativity.

Turns out, those shared interests turned into shared laughs. Then friendships. Then, a support system he didn't even know he needed.

When you have ADHD and anxiety, you often feel isolated—not because you lack social skills, but because making and maintaining connections can feel exhausting. But the right environments can make connection feel easy.

So, how can you find your people? Maybe:

- Join a class, league, or club around a hobby you enjoy (no perfection required)
- Use apps like Meetup, Bumble BFF, or Discord groups to find like-minded folks
- Volunteer for a cause you care about, it creates connection with purpose
- Attend community events like local festivals, library talks, open mic nights.

New connections aren't about being impressive. They're about being present.

Practicing Vulnerability

The people who really connect with you aren't looking for perfection. They're looking for truth.

One of Noah's biggest breakthroughs came during a conversation with a new friend. They were talking about focus and motivation, and instead of brushing off his challenges, Noah said: "Honestly? Most days I feel like I'm running uphill in my own mind."

His friend paused. Then nodded. Then said: "Same."

That moment cracked something open. A wall fell down. And from that space, trust began. Being vulnerable doesn't mean you spill your guts to strangers. It means you stop pretending everything's fine when it's not.

Exercise: Practice Authentic Connection

Connection lives in the space between being seen and letting others feel seen too. Give the following a try:

- Share how you're really doing with someone you

trust.

- Replace "I'm good" with something more real: "Today's been hard, but I'm getting through it."
- Ask others deeper questions: "What's been on your mind lately?" or "What's something you're excited about?"
- In conversations, focus on active listening: Put the phone down, hold eye contact, reflect back what you hear.

Building Conflict Resolution Skills

Every close relationship will hit friction. It's not a matter of if—it's when.

Noah used to avoid conflict at all costs. He'd shut down, ghost, or change the subject. But it only built resentment and distance.

In therapy, he learned a new approach:

- Start with feelings, not blame.
- Listen to understand, not to win.

- Look for shared goals, not separate sides.

It wasn't always easy. But it turned arguments into conversations. And those conversations built stronger trust.

Check out these tools for conflict growth:

- Use "I" statements: "I feel overwhelmed when plans change last-minute, and I'd love more heads-up."
- Practice empathetic reflection: "What I hear you saying is..."
- When emotions run hot, pause and revisit later rather than escalate
- After resolution, reflect together: "What worked here? What could we do better next time?"

Working through hard moments with care builds resilience—together.

Meaningful connection isn't about having a hundred friends. It's about building a few relationships where you can be fully human—messy, growing, and real.

Wrapping It Up: The Power of Choosing Forward

By now, you've done something that many never will—you've looked inward, faced hard truths, and taken real steps toward change. That's not small. That's courageous.

Noah didn't transform overnight. He still gets distracted. Still wrestles with doubt. But now, he has tools, structure, and support. He's not chasing control—he's creating direction.

You are, too.

Every time you set a boundary...

Every time you reflect instead of react...

Every time you show up for your goals, your relationships, or your own peace of mind...

You're rewriting the narrative. You're becoming the kind of man who leads with purpose, focus, and heart.

And if there's one truth to carry forward, it's this: You don't have to do it all to change everything. You just have to keep choosing forward—one step, one choice, one honest effort at a time.

Your growth doesn't stop here. This is just where momentum begins. You've got this. And you've got more in you than you ever thought possible.

10

CONCLUSION: YOU MADE IT—AND THAT MATTERS

"Success is not final, failure is not fatal: it is the courage to continue that counts." – Winston Churchill

I want you to pause for a moment and reflect on everything you've just accomplished. You didn't just flip through the pages of a book. You faced your fears and insecurities. You didn't settle for complaining, feeling stuck, or resigning yourself to life as it is—you took action and got to work. And that already sets you apart and deserves recognition.

Most people remain trapped in the cycle of frustration, hoping life will magically get easier. But not you. You've dedicated time and energy to understanding your ADHD and your anxiety. You've taken a close look at your habits, your thoughts, and your emotions—even the ones usually tucked away in the back of the drawer.

I congratulate you on your effort and your strength.

Let's take a moment to review everything you've worked on:

- You've learned how ADHD and anxiety intertwine in men's lives, and how they often hide behind distraction, anger, procrastination, or emotional shutdown.

- You've explored tools like CBT, mindfulness, visualization, and breathing techniques to calm your mind and focus your attention.

- You've practiced how to set boundaries, manage your time like a pro, and stay present and engaged when negative thoughts try to take over.

- You've courageously faced emotional regulation and social anxiety head-on.

- You've created space for self-compassion and self-care—things that don't always come naturally but make all the difference.

- And perhaps most importantly: you've started to build a life that supports and encourages your personal growth—not just your survival.

And when you look back at this list of accomplishments, you can't help but feel deeply proud of yourself—and that's something truly important.

This isn't the end. What you've gained isn't just knowledge—it's a toolbox you've built with your own effort. It's yours to carry with you, to lean on when life becomes chaotic, noisy, or overwhelming. And remember, the more you practice using these tools, the more instinctive and natural they'll become.

Life won't always be easy. At times, it will get messy, confusing, and there will be moments that test your limits. But now you're prepared. You've trained your mind. You've strengthened your self-awareness. You've built strategies that actually work.

When those low moments come—and make no mistake, they will—pause. Breathe. Then visualize the life you're building. Picture the calm you want in your home, the connection you want in your relationships, the purpose you long for in your work. Let that vision ground you and guide you. You have tools. You have clarity. You have resilience. Stay steady. You're ready.

You also have a future that is entirely yours to shape—like a block of marble in the hands of a sculptor. And now, you've developed the clarity, the confidence, and the emotional strength to carve something meaningful. With each steady stroke, you're creating a life that reflects your values, your vision, and your growth.

One last thing: if this book helped you, I'd love for you to leave a review. Your story might inspire another man to take that same first step you once took—and that could change everything for him.

As you close this final page, I encourage you to stay curious, and to keep treating yourself with kindness. And above all, keep going—one choice, one breath, one step at a time. You've already proven you have what it takes to move forward, and your next chapter is waiting.

I HAVE SOMETHING SPECIAL FOR YOU!

Do you want to be among the first to read my next book... completely FREE?

Just scan the code below and join my readers' club.

Inside, amazing surprises await you: early access to my latest releases, free audiobooks, signed copies, and many more gifts!

Did you enjoy this book?

Your opinion can make a difference.

As an independent author, I don't have a big publishing house or marketing campaigns behind me. What I do have is you. And every time you leave a review, you're helping more people discover this book.

If it helped you, made you think, brought a smile to your face, or accompanied you through a tough time... I'd love for you to share that with others. It doesn't have to be long, just honest:

- What did you like the most?
- Who do you think this book could help?
- What would you have liked to see included?

Thank you for being there. Your review not only helps me—it could also inspire other readers.

OTHER BOOKS BY NOAH J. NOLAN

www.ingramcontent.com/pod-product-compliance
Lightning Source LLC
LaVergne TN
LVHW100104250926
848814LV00045B/19

9789916781944